GAOZHONG YINGYU YUEDU
WENBEN JIEDU YU JIAOXUE ZHIDAO

高中英语阅读文本解读与教学指导

6

主编 葛炳芳

人民教育出版社
·北京·

图书在版编目（CIP）数据

高中英语阅读文本解读与教学指导 . 6 / 葛炳芳主编 . — 北京：人民教育出版社，2023.1
ISBN 978-7-107-37149-3

Ⅰ . ①高… Ⅱ . ①葛… Ⅲ . ①英语—阅读教学—高中—教学参考资料 Ⅳ . ① G633.413

中国国家版本馆 CIP 数据核字（2023）第 002103 号

高中英语阅读文本解读与教学指导　6

出版发行	人民教育出版社
	（北京市海淀区中关村南大街 17 号院 1 号楼　邮编：100081）
网　　址	http://www.pep.com.cn
经　　销	全国新华书店
印　　刷	北京天宇星印刷厂
版　　次	2023 年 1 月第 1 版
印　　次	2023 年 2 月第 1 次印刷
开　　本	890 毫米 × 1 240 毫米　1/16
印　　张	8.5
字　　数	196 千字
定　　价	41.90 元

版权所有·未经许可不得采用任何方式擅自复制或使用本产品任何部分·违者必究
如发现内容质量问题、印装质量问题，请与本社联系。电话：400-810-5788

主　　编：葛炳芳

作　　者：梁美珍　陈　帅　管健伟　黄凌辰　潘仙琴　张　芳　江淑芳
　　　　　李　琦　唐思峰　余璃明　邱　玲　王思颖　严佩华　黄　科
　　　　　沈一频　马瑾辰
　　　　　（按单元作者的先后顺序）

责任编辑： 陆珂米

版式设计： 于　艳

封面设计： 于　艳

前　言

亲爱的读者，您是否认为解读阅读文本很重要却常常无从下手？您是否想帮助学生更好地理解文本却总觉得缺乏思路？您是否感到阅读教学中语言的处理很困难又很无趣？您是否认为阅读教学中应该训练写作能力但做起来却费时费力、收效甚微？您是否认为学生思维能力的提升只能是一个"自我发展"的过程？您是否认为阅读教学不该总是按照某种程式化的套路开展？您是否认为面对英语基础薄弱的学生，在阅读课上只能领着他们读读单词和译译句子，而无法进行思维和写作训练？您是否认为阅读教学中的主线意识很关键却在教学设计中常常无主线可循？……

如果您有以上的困惑或者疑虑，那么让我们告诉您：不要焦虑，《高中英语阅读文本解读与教学指导》丛书（以下简称《文本解读与教学指导》）出版了！这是专门为人教版《普通高中教科书 英语》（必修 第一册至第三册、选择性必修 第一册至第四册）"阅读与思考"（Reading and Thinking）板块的文本编写的教学案例集。本套丛书一共七册，教学案例对应学生用书各个单元的主篇阅读。每个单元由文本解读、通用版教学案例、提高版教学案例三大部分构成。其中，文本解读中的"总体解读"重点聚焦文本的主旨、文体和阅读策略；"段落解读"以问题为导向，从内容、思维和语言三个维度解读文本；"综合解读"则是以教学设计为目的的文本解读。

考虑到学生的差异性，我们提供了通用版和提高版两个层次的教学案例。除必修第一册的过渡单元（Welcome Unit）外，每个单元每一层次的阅读课都按两个课时设计教学。每课时均包括课时目标、设计思路、教学过程和教学反思四个主要部分。"课时目标"按"用什么方法设计什么活动以达成什么目标"的思路呈现。"设计思路"提供一个整体的教学设计框架。"教学过程"不仅呈现了细致的教学步骤，还特别强调教学活动与课时目标的关联性、设计意图和核心素养提升点。如果教学活动涉及整体的口头或书面产出，本书则尽可能提供教师的参考范本。"教学反思"是教师基于实际授课情况进行的、带有自我评价性质的思考，目的在于总结成功之处、反思存在的问题以及提出改进的思路和方法。此外，需要说明的是：对于两个版本的教学案例，本书均配有相对应的教学录像，供感兴趣的读者参考、使用。

本套教学案例集遵循《普通高中英语课程标准（2017年版）》以及根据此课程标准编写的人教版高中英语教材的教学理念，并基于获得"2018年国家级基础教育成果奖"一等奖的《基于综合视野的英语阅读教学改进行动》研究成果创作而成，这也是人民教育出版社课程教材研究所"十三五"立项课题《基于综合视野的高中英语阅读课堂教学改进行动》（KC2017—002）的研究成果。

编写本套教学案例集的主要目的是研讨阅读文本解读的重要性和常态阅读教学的综合性，为一线教师的日常教学提供可借鉴的教学案例。课题组编写时的核心考量可以概括为四个方面，即challenge、opportunity、responsibility和emancipation，这四个方面可简称为"CORE"。

Challenge（挑战）：课题组直面常态教学中存在的实际问题，努力以内容、思维、语言有机融合的理念破解英语阅读教学中不够重视思维训练、内容与语言"两张皮"等难题；不刻意追求"表面繁荣"的虚假课堂教学，而是坚持常态的、真实的课堂教学。在设计和录制课例的时候，"真实"是此课题最重要的考量。为此，所有的教学案例都配有录像，供读者研究、评判。

Opportunity（时机）：已有的关于阅读教学的研究，让研究者有机会逐步深入地实践"英语阅读教学的综合视野"的理念，在一次次真实的、常态的课例实践中找寻改进日常阅读教学的时机。《文本解读与教学指导》系列丛书的出版，有效地促进了我们践行"教而有研，研而促教"的信条，并为广大教师改进教学和研究提供了素材。

Responsibility（责任）：广大教师和教研员有责任不断提升自己的教育理念，改进自己的教学实践，多从学生的视角思考现有的课堂教学，尽最大努力帮助学生达成最好的学习效果。在《文本解读与教学指导》系列丛书中，教师会就同一教学材料，针对不同学生设计不同的教学任务，搭建不同的教学支架，尽可能平衡各种教学要素，踏踏实实地完成好每个教学步骤，力求达到最佳的教学效果。

Emancipation（解放）：本研究直面挑战，把握真实教研的时机，担起促进学生真正学习的责任，给读者呈现值得研究、探讨的原生态教学案例，目的是促进广大教师在专业上的真正成长。我们无意给这些案例贴上"示范课""优质课"之类的标签，它们还远远不是这样的课。但是，这些基于研究而呈现的真实、扎实、平实的案例，是真正促进读者思考、研究、评判和专业成长的好材料。只有教师成为善于反思的实践者，才能让教学更自由，让学习更自主。

这一项目的顺利推进，得益于人民教育出版社英语编辑室的大力支持。从项目立项到文稿编辑，他们的支持无时不在。作为主编，我还要感谢我的团队，他们深读文本、精心磨课、不计得失、贡献智慧。此外，我也要诚挚地感谢参与录课的学校和师生们的大力支持。

本册的主要编写人员如下（每个单元第一人为组长）。

Unit 1：梁美珍、陈帅、管健伟、黄凌辰。通用版阅读课由陈帅老师执教，学生来自浙江省台州市双语高级中学；提高版阅读课由黄凌辰老师执教，学生来自浙江省台州市第一中学。

Unit 2：潘仙琴、张芳、江淑芳。通用版阅读课由江淑芳老师执教，学生来自浙江省金华市芙蓉外国语学校；提高版阅读课由张芳老师执教，学生来自浙江师范大学附属中学。

Unit 3：李琦、唐思峰、余璃明。通用版阅读课由余璃明老师执教，学生来自江西省南昌市朝阳中学；提高版阅读课由唐思峰老师执教，学生来自江西省南昌市第二中学。

Unit 4：邱玲、王思颖、严佩华。通用版阅读课由丘玲老师执教，学生来自广东省广州市南海中学；提高版阅读课由严佩华老师执教，学生来自广东广雅中学。

Unit 5：黄科、沈一频、马瑾辰。通用版阅读课由马瑾辰老师执教，学生来自浙江省杭州市长征中学；提高版阅读课由黄科老师执教，学生来自浙江省杭州第二中学。

学生用书中的"阅读与思考"板块的文本是普通高中英语阅读教学中最核心的资源。我们期待所呈现的普通却很真实的课堂教学案例能给广大一线教师朋友带来思考和收获，同时也真诚欢迎大家通过邮箱learningabc@126.com提出您的宝贵意见，以便我们进一步改进。

葛炳芳

2021年盛夏

于杭州西溪

CONTENTS

UNIT 1 ART — 1
第一节　文本解读 — 1
第二节　通用版教学案例 — 9
第三节　提高版教学案例 — 16

UNIT 2 HEALTHY LIFESTYLE — 23
第一节　文本解读 — 23
第二节　通用版教学案例 — 30
第三节　提高版教学案例 — 39

UNIT 3 ENVIRONMENTAL PROTECTION — 48
第一节　文本解读 — 48
第二节　通用版教学案例 — 54
第三节　提高版教学案例 — 64

UNIT 4 ADVERSITY AND COURAGE — 71
第一节　文本解读 — 71
第二节　通用版教学案例 — 78
第三节　提高版教学案例 — 85

UNIT 5 POEMS — 93
第一节　文本解读 — 93
第二节　通用版教学案例 — 101
第三节　提高版教学案例 — 114

UNIT 1 ART
Reading and Thinking　A SHORT HISTORY OF WESTERN PAINTING

第一节　文本解读

一、总体解读

本单元的主题是"艺术"。阅读文本"A Short History of Western Painting"通过介绍几个世纪以来西方绘画艺术的发展变化，在帮助学生了解西方绘画艺术简史的同时，引发学生对于艺术本质和价值的深层追问和思考。

该文本是一篇典型的知识性小品文。作者用清晰的结构和客观的语言，以西方绘画艺术发展过程中的四个主要时期为序，以每个时期的著名画家及其主要作品为代表，简要介绍了西方绘画艺术在主题、题材和技巧三个方面的发展变化，揭示了西方绘画艺术发展的历史和社会原因。艺术源于生活，又高于生活；艺术反映意识，意识又助推艺术发展；艺术在一代又一代艺术家对"What is art?"的追问和探索中得以传承、创新和发展。

全文共八段。第一段是引言，首句设问"什么是西方艺术？"，然后以"学习西方绘画艺术的发展史或许是理解西方艺术的最好方式"来作答，引入话题，揭示写作目的。第二至第八段是主体部分，由四个小标题引导，按照西方绘画艺术发展的四个主要时期依次展开。第二段介绍了中世纪绘画作品主要为传教服务，呈现出"原始、二维"的绘画特点；13世纪画家乔托的出现改变了这一现象，他的作品展示了真实人物。第三至第五段介绍了文艺复兴时期绘画艺术的特点。与之前的画家主要关注宗教主题不同，这个时期的画家更加关注身边的人和世界。同时，随着透视画法和油画的出现，绘画作品变得更加写实。第六和第七段介绍了在印象派时期，由于摄影术的发明，人们不再需要通过绘画作品来保留人与世界的模样。画家必须找到一种新的方式来看待他们的艺术，于是他们开始关注物象给人们带来的主观印象和内心感受。第八段简要概括了在现代艺术时期，多种流派同时存在。虽然画家们对绘画艺术的理解和表达不同，但他们对艺术本质的追求一直没有停歇。全文以"什么是艺术？"这一问题结尾，首尾呼应，引发思考。

在阅读策略方面，教师可引导学生通过关注大标题、小标题、插图以及其他语篇布局特征，获知文本体裁和结构；引导学生通过了解篇首设问导入等写作手法，领悟作者的写作意图；引导学生通过关注词句的表意功能、句子之间以及段落之间的衔接，了解西方绘画艺术发展的相关知识；最后引导学生通过梳理归纳西方绘画艺术发展过程中的"变"与"不变"，理解推动艺术发展的重要因素，展开对"什么是艺术？"的思考，培养批判性思维能力。

二、段落解读

表1：分段解读

The original text	Interpretation
A SHORT HISTORY OF WESTERN PAINTING	**1. What are the key words in the title?** Western painting, history. **2. What pops into your mind when you see the words "Western painting"? What are some aspects of and facts about Western painting?** Styles, famous painters, famous paintings, social development, etc. **3. What do you think of when you read the word "history" in the title?** Development, change, etc. **4. What do you think the text will tell you?** (Answers will vary.)
What is Western art? It is hard to give a precise definition. As there have been so many different styles of Western art, it is impossible to describe them all in a short text. Perhaps the best way to understand Western art is to look at the development of Western painting over the centuries.	**1. Why does the writer ask a question at the beginning of the text?** To attract the readers' attention and to lead into the topic. It is often an effective technique for expository writing. **2. Does the writer offer a precise answer to the question? Why?** No, because it is hard to give a precise definition, and it is impossible to describe so many different styles of Western art in a short text. **3. What does the writer suggest doing?** Looking at the development of Western painting over the centuries. **4. How will the following paragraphs probably be organised?** Most probably in a chronological order. **5. What purpose does the first paragraph serve?** To involve the readers in the topic and convey the writer's writing intention.

续表

The original text	Interpretation
The Middle Ages (from the 5th to the 15th century) During the Middle Ages, the purpose of Western art was to teach people about Christianity. Thus, artists were not interested in painting realistic scenes. Their works were often primitive and two-dimensional, and the main characters were often made much larger than everyone else to show their importance. This began to change in the 13th century with Giotto di Bondone (1267–1337). While his paintings still had religious themes, they showed real people in a real environment. In particular, his paintings are set apart from other paintings by their realistic human faces and deep emotional impact.	**1. What most probably best reflects the values of the Western world during the Middle Ages? Why do you think so?** Christianity. The purpose of Western art at that time was to teach people about this religion, so it must have been very important. **2. What were the paintings like?** They were primitive and two-dimensional, and the main characters were often painted much larger than everyone else to show their importance. **3. Did the paintings stay the same throughout the period? How did you know?** No, because the text says "This began to change in the 13th century …". **4. Who is mentioned as the first painter to lead in the change?** Giotto di Bondone (1267–1337). **5. How did his paintings compare to the previous style?** His paintings still had religious themes, but showed real people in a real environment. **6. How does the writer show the development of Western painting during the period?** By comparison and contrast. (1) The writer uses the sentence structure "While … still …" to show that although the themes of Giotto's paintings were still religious, the characters he painted looked more realistic. (2) The writer uses the phrase "set apart from … by …" to indicate the contrast of Giotto's particular painting style.
The Renaissance (from the 14th to the 17th century) New ideas and values gradually replaced old ones from the Middle Ages. As a result, painters concentrated less on religious themes. They began to adopt a more	**1. What is the function of the first sentence in this paragraph?** To serve as a transitional sentence that connects the two periods, explaining the cause of the development between them.

The original text	Interpretation
humanistic attitude to life. An important breakthrough during this period was the use of perspective by Masaccio (1401–1428). Influential painters such as Leonardo da Vinci (1452–1519), Michelangelo (1475–1564), and Raphael (1483–1520) built upon Giotto and Masaccio's innovations to produce some of the greatest art that Europe had ever seen.	**2. What development did it bring about as a consequence?** Painters paid less attention to religious themes and began to show a more humanistic attitude towards life. **3. How does the writer support his statement?** By giving examples. One of the examples is the use of perspective by Masaccio (1401–1428), which is the art of creating an effect of depth and distance in a picture by representing people and things that are far away as being smaller than those that are closer to the artist. **4. Why are Giotto and Masaccio both mentioned in the last sentence?** To show that famous painters were influenced by them, indicating the relationship between inheritance and innovation.
Another innovation was the use of oil paints. With their deep colours and realism, some of the best oil paintings look like photographs. While painters as early as Da Vinci had used oil, this technique reached its height with Rembrandt (1606–1669), who gained a reputation as a master of shadow and light.	**1. What is the word "another" in this paragraph used for?** It is meant to offer a second example to support the writer's idea in the previous paragraph. **2. What writing technique does the writer employ to describe oil painting to us?** Simile. The writer uses "like" to compare oil paintings to photographs to show the resemblance between them, such as their deep colours and realism. **3. Who was recognised as a master of shadow and light? How did he become so good at it?** Rembrandt (1606–1669). He built upon influential painters like Da Vinci to develop his technique, echoing the relationship between inheritance and innovation.

续表

The original text	Interpretation
In subject matter, the emphasis increasingly shifted from religious themes to people and the world around us. Kings, nobles, and people of high rank wanted to purchase accurate pictures of themselves and the people they loved. Others wanted paintings showing important historical events or stories from mythology. Finally, most clients wanted paintings that were beautiful and interesting to look at.	**1. Which word has a similar meaning to "change" in this paragraph? How did you know?** Shift; the word is followed by the expression "from … to …". **2. What developed besides the painting techniques? How did it develop?** The subject matter of Western paintings. It changed from religious themes to people and the world around us. **3. How does the writer support his idea?** By giving examples of different people's choice of subject matter. **4. What does "finally" suggest in this paragraph?** It indicates the end of the writer's supporting examples and also the paragraph. **5. How does the writer organise the three paragraphs about the Renaissance? Are they well related to each other?** The first two sentences in Paragraph 3 state the cause and result of the development of Western painting from the Middle Ages to the Renaissance. To illustrate the development, the writer includes two innovations in painting techniques (the use of perspective in Paragraph 3 and the use of oil paints in Paragraph 4) and the shift in the subject matter of paintings (in Paragraph 5, showing the changes from religious themes to people and the world around us).
Impressionism (late 19th to early 20th century) The development of Western art slowed until the invention of photography in the mid-19th century. After that, paintings were no longer needed to preserve what people and the world looked like. Hence, painters had to find a new way of looking at their art.	**1. Why is the invention of photography mentioned at the beginning of this paragraph?** To provide background information on the development of Western painting in this period. This invention changed the slow development of painting. The expression "… slowed until …" tells the reader that the "slowing" stopped when the invention appeared.

The original text	Interpretation
From this, Impressionism emerged in France. The name of this new movement came from the painting by Claude Monet (1840–1926) called *Impression, Sunrise*. In this work, Monet's aim was to convey the light and movement in the scene—the subjective impression the scene gave him—but not a detailed record of the scene itself.	**2. What contributed to the development of Western art?** With photographs replacing the function of paintings to preserve images of people and the world, painters had to find a new way to look at art. **3. How did the new movement get its name?** From Claude Monet's painting called *Impression, Sunrise*. **4. Which word describes an important aspect of Impressionism? What do you understand by it?** Subjective. What each painting conveys is the subjective impression the scene gives to the artist, which is based on feelings rather than accurate details.
While many impressionists painted scenes of nature or daily life, others, such as Renoir (1841–1919), focused on people. Unlike the cold, black-and-white photographs of that time period, Renoir's paintings are full of light, shadow, colour, and life. He sought to show not just the outer image of his subjects, but their inner warmth and humanity as well.	**1. How does the writer introduce another development in Impressionist painting?** The writer uses the sentence structure "While ..., ..." to contrast the painting subjects of painters like Claude Monet, who painted scenes, and painters like Renoir, who focused on people. **2. What contributions did Renoir make?** (1) He extended Impressionism to also focus on people, rather than just nature or daily life. (2) He enriched his paintings to show not only the outer image of people but also their inner warmth and humanity. **3. How does the writer show Renoir's contributions to the development of Western painting?** By comparison and contrast. The writer uses the sentence structures "Unlike ..." and "not just ... but ... as well" to make comparisons and contrasts between photographs and Renoir's style of painting.
Modern Art (from the 20th century to today) After Impressionism, subsequent artists began to ask, "What do we do next?" Painters such as Picasso	**1. How did artists develop Western art after Impressionism?** Painters such as Picasso (1881–1973) tried to examine the shapes existing in the natural world, with Cubism. Others painted in a realistic but dream-like

续表

The original text	Interpretation
(1881–1973) tried to analyse the shapes which existed in the natural world but in a new way, with Cubism. Others gave their paintings a realistic but dream-like quality. Still others turned to abstract art. What they attempted to do was no longer show reality, but instead to ask the question, "What is art?"	way. Still others devoted themselves to abstract art. **2. What did they attempt to do?** They enthusiastically explored new ways to express art, thus making Western art further develop. **3. Could artists possibly find the answer to the question "What is art?"** There is no fixed answer to the question. **4. How will Western art develop in the future?** (Answers will vary.)

表2：跨段解读

Putting it all together
1. What periods are mentioned to explain the development of Western painting? The Middle Ages (from the 5th to the 15th century); The Renaissance (from the 14th to the 17th century); Impressionism (from the late 19th to early 20th century); Modern Art (from the 20th century to today). **2. How has Western painting developed and who are some representative painters from each period?** In the Middle Ages, paintings were mostly Christianity-themed. Then Giotto di Bondone (1267–1337) began to include realistic scenes. In the Renaissance, painters concentrated less on religious themes and adopted a more humanistic attitude to life. The use of perspective was first adopted by Masaccio (1401–1428). And the use of oil paints helped Rembrandt (1606–1669) gain a reputation as a master of shadow and light. These two developments were important innovations in painting techniques during this period. The subject matter of the paintings also shifted from religious themes to people and the world around us. In Impressionism, Claude Monet (1840–1926) tried to convey the subjective impression that scenes gave him, while Renoir (1841–1919) sought to show not only the outer image of people but also their inner warmth and humanity. In Modern Art, painters such as Picasso (1881–1973) have attempted to explore new ways to express art. The development of Western art is sure to continue. **3. What caused the development of Western painting?** New ideas and values replaced old ones. Also, with the invention of photography, painting lost some of its value, so artists became devoted to finding new ways to express art.

续表

Putting it all together

4. Is the text well organised? What techniques are employed?
With the question "What is Western art?" raised at the very beginning of the text, coupled with the echoing question "What is art?" at the very end of the text, the writer intends to help readers understand Western art by looking at the development of Western painting over the centuries. To illustrate the development clearly, the writer organises the text in the order of time. The writer also uses techniques such as giving examples, making comparisons and contrasts, showing causes and results, and providing a simile, which all make the text logical, cohesive, and credible.

5. What is (Western) art according to the text? What is your understanding of art after reading the text?
(Answers will vary.)

三、综合解读

综合上述分析，我们对文本进行教学设计时，应着重考量以下三个方面。

1. 语言学习

本单元阅读文本的语言学习可围绕"the development of Western painting"这个话题语境展开。教师可基于此话题语境展开教学设计，引导学生梳理与"绘画"主题相关的词汇，如 style、painter、painting、master、work、primitive、two-dimensional、realistic、humanistic、subjective、abstract 等；梳理表达"变化"的词汇，如 emerge、begin to change ...、replace、build upon、shift from ... to ...、be set apart from、development、breakthrough、innovation、gradually、increasingly 等；梳理关于"比较和对比"的词汇，如 While ... still ...、less ... more ...、... but not ...、not just ... but ... as well、... but instead ... 等。教师要引导学生通过语言学习理解文本，并且结合话题语境和语言功能积累语言知识。

2. 思维培养

在思维培养方面，教师可借助"西方绘画艺术发展"这条主线来设计教学活动。教师可引导学生通过梳理不同时期代表性画家及其引领的艺术发展成就，把握不同时期的绘画风格，了解西方绘画艺术发展的相关知识，形成系统思维；通过关注句子之间以及段落之间的衔接，探寻推动西方绘画艺术发展的重要因素，思考艺术发展中传承与创新之间的辩证关系，培养逻辑思维能力；通过评析作者的写作技巧，培养批判性思维能力；通过赏析西方经典绘画作品及有关艺术的名家名言，拉近与艺术之间的距离，展开对艺术内涵与价值的思考；通过模仿名言造句，培养创造性思维能力。

3. 文化意识

通过阅读和理解文本，学生可以了解西方绘画艺术发展历程，把握不同时期西方绘画作品的特色。教师还应引导学生通过赏析经典绘画作品和名家名言，认识艺术的价值，感悟艺术的魅力，学会在生活中感知美、追求美、创造美。

第二节 通用版教学案例

教学内容安排：第一课时帮助学生整体理解文本内容，梳理文本结构；第二课时引导学生根据文本信息，探寻推动西方绘画艺术发展的重要因素，赏析不同时期的绘画作品，加深对绘画艺术的认知。

第一课时

一、课时目标

1. 通过浏览部分西方绘画作品，激活背景知识。
2. 通过浏览大标题和小标题，识别文本特征，概括文本大意，厘清文本结构。
3. 通过阅读和探究，了解西方绘画艺术的发展历程，体会重点语言的运用。

二、设计思路

本节课以帮助学生通过细读文本了解西方绘画艺术的发展历程为重点展开。教师首先呈现不同时期的西方绘画作品，引入话题，引导学生谈论自己最喜欢的作品；接着让学生浏览全文，根据大标题、小标题等信息厘清文本结构；随后引导学生开展三次自主阅读，梳理不同时期代表性画家的基本信息，理解他们在推动西方绘画艺术发展中发挥的作用；最后引导学生以时间轴为线，从主题、题材和技巧三个方面探究西方绘画艺术发展历程，逐步加深对西方绘画艺术的认知和理解。

三、教学过程

Activity 1: Viewing and talking about Western paintings

本活动旨在落实课时目标1。

Look at six Western paintings and choose your favourite one and introduce it.

【设计意图】让学生浏览几幅不同时期的西方绘画作品，引导学生初步赏析不同风格的西方绘画艺术。

【核心素养提升点】提升学生的语言表达能力。

Activity 2: Outlining the development of Western painting

本活动旨在落实课时目标2。

1. **Read the title and think about the writing order.**
2. **Read the subtitles and figure out the structure and main idea of the text.**

Q1: How many periods of time are introduced in the text? What are they?

Q2: What's the function of Paragraph 1?

Q3: What's the main idea of the text?

【设计意图】引导学生通过浏览大标题和小标题，熟悉话题，把握文本大意，厘清文本结构。

【核心素养提升点】培养学生读和看（viewing）的能力；提升学生概括信息的能力。

Activity 3: Reading and exploring the role of important painters in the development of Western painting

本活动旨在落实课时目标3。

1. Read the text and answer the following questions.

Q1: Who are the painters mentioned in the four periods?

Q2: What information about the painters is introduced?

T: Circle the names of the painters and bracket the information about them.

【设计意图】引导学生阅读文本，获取四个时期代表性画家的基本信息，为进一步梳理西方绘画艺术的发展做铺垫。

【核心素养提升点】提升学生识别和整理关键信息的能力。

2. Read the text and figure out the importance of the painters in the development of Western painting.

Q: Why are these painters introduced in each period?

T: Find the sentences that show these painters helped change Western painting. Some of you may find this task a little bit difficult. In order to help you, here is the tip on page 2 of the Student Book, "Identify change".

【设计意图】引导学生自主阅读，关注表达"变化"的语言，梳理并理解四个时期的代表性画家对推动西方绘画艺术发展所起的作用。该任务难度略大，学生自主阅读后可与同伴讨论。

【核心素养提升点】帮助学生理解语言的表意功能；提升学生分析信息的能力。

Activity 4: Introducing the development of Western painting

本活动旨在落实课时目标3。

Read the text and work in groups to introduce how Western painting developed over the four periods from one of these three aspects: theme, subject, or technique.

Q: How did Western painting develop over the four periods? Please choose one aspect, theme, subject, or technique, to introduce it.

【设计意图】引导学生开展合作学习，依托文本信息，以时间轴为线梳理西方绘画艺术发展历程。

【核心素养提升点】提升学生合作探究的能力；培养学生整合信息的能力。

Assignment

1. Read the text three times to better understand the development of Western painting.
2. Recite three sentences that you like.

【设计意图】引导学生复习课堂所学，赏析文本语言；引导学生养成欣赏、背诵美句的良好习惯。

【核心素养提升点】提升学生的语言感知能力。

四、教学反思

本节课教学以学生自主阅读和探究为主，以教师设问和追问为辅。教师以文本中最容易引起读者关注的各个时期代表性画家为切入点，引导学生提取与代表性画家相关的信息（如Who、What和Why），梳理西方绘画艺术在主题、题材和技巧三个方面的发展变化。这个过程降低了阅读难度，帮助学生通过反复阅读理解内容、品味语言、提升思维能力。

本节课存在几点不足之处。首先，在活动3的第二个阅读环节，有学生只关注了表达"变化"的句子，并未关注该句是否能够说明某位画家积极推动了西方绘画艺术的发展。教师在给出课堂指令时，应点明要学生寻找各个时期代表性画家推动西方绘画艺术发展的相关语句，或者在学生回答的时候进行更加清晰的引导。其次，在活动4的小组呈现环节，由于时间不够，学生未能从主题、题材和技巧三个方面多角度探究和理解西方绘画艺术的发展。教师应更加合理地安排各个环节的教学时间。最后，本节课板书只在活动4中呈现了有关西方绘画艺术发展的核心关键词，呈现时机偏晚，内容也稍显单薄。教师可在前面环节板书更多表达"变化"的单词和词块，以帮助学生加深对这些词汇的理解。

第二课时

一、课时目标

1. 通过分享自己喜欢的语句欣赏文本语言，同时回顾西方绘画艺术发展的几个时期。
2. 通过关注句子之间以及段落之间的衔接，探究推动西方绘画艺术发展的重要因素，更深入理解西方绘画艺术的发展历程。
3. 通过辨别和赏析绘画作品，重温西方绘画艺术发展历程，整合文本信息和语言，在真实语境中实现对语言的迁移和运用。

二、设计思路

本节课以引导学生分析和理解推动西方绘画艺术发展的重要因素和赏析不同时期的绘画作品为重点展开，旨在帮助学生深入理解不同时期西方绘画艺术的发展，并通过实际应用，内化所学语言。教师首先引导学生交流课后作业，分享自己欣赏的语句，并结合文本内容，谈论自己喜欢的西方绘画艺术类型；然后引导学生根据文本信息，探讨在不同时期推动西方绘画艺术发展的重要因素；最后引导学生运用表达"变化"的相关语言，辨别和赏析不同时期的绘画作品，发展综合思维，提高语言表达能力。

三、教学过程

Activity 1: Talking about one period of Western painting

本活动旨在落实课时目标1。

1. **Share your favourite sentence.**
2. **Share your favourite period of Western painting.**

【设计意图】引导学生通过交流课后作业，简单回顾上节课内容，做好两节课之间的衔接。

【核心素养提升点】提升学生的语言表达能力。

Activity 2: Reading and exploring the reasons for the development of Western painting

本活动旨在落实课时目标2。

Read the text and figure out the reasons for the development of Western painting over the four periods.

Q1: Can you find some connected sentences that can infer the reasons for the development of Western painting?

Q2: What caused the development of Western painting over the centuries?

【设计意图】引导学生通过文本阅读关注句子之间以及段落之间的衔接，探讨在不同时期推动西方绘画艺术发展的重要因素。

【核心素养提升点】培养学生抓住文本叙事逻辑的能力；提升学生阐释深层问题的能力。

Activity 3: Identifying and introducing the paintings

本活动旨在落实课时目标3。

1. **Figure out the painters of each painting.**

Q1: Which painters painted the paintings?

Q2: What do you think of the paintings?

2. **Appreciate paintings.**

T: Suppose you are a volunteer at a Western painting exhibition. Please introduce one of the four paintings to visitors from at least three aspects.

【设计意图】步骤1引导学生基于对不同时期西方绘画艺术发展以及相关画家的理解，初步辨别、赏析几幅绘画作品。步骤2引导学生对代表性画作进行多角度赏析，综合检测学生对不同时期西方绘画艺术发展的理解，包括在某个时期推动绘画艺术发展的重要因素，绘画艺术在主题、题材和技巧三个方面的变化，以及相关画家在推动绘画艺术发展中所起的重要作用等。教师可提供语言输出的框架及与"变化"相关的语言表达，引导学生关注语言运用。

【核心素养提升点】提升学生的语篇分析能力；增强学生的综合语言运用能力。

Assignment

1. Please finish Activity 3 (page 3, Student Book).
2. Choose one of the paintings and write down your explanation logically.

> In my opinion, the first/second/third/fourth painting belongs to ... The reasons are as follows.
>
> First, in subject matter, ... Besides, as for how it was painted, ... Finally, the purpose of it is to / its aim is to / it attempts to / it seeks to ...
>
> Thus, I'm convinced that ...

【设计意图】引导学生根据框架，从主题、题材和技巧三个方面对一幅绘画作品进行分析，巩固本课所学语言，加深对不同时期西方绘画艺术发展的理解。

【核心素养提升点】培养学生的综合分析能力；提升学生的语言表达能力。

The teacher's version:

In my opinion, the fourth painting belongs to the Renaissance. The reasons are as follows.

First, in subject matter, this painting is set apart from other paintings by its realistic character. Besides, as for how it was painted, it looks like a photograph and was painted with deep colours and realism. It also shows one of the innovations of the Renaissance period—the use of oil paints. Finally, the painting attempts to convey a more humanistic attitude to life.

Thus, I'm convinced that this painting belongs to the Renaissance.

附: Worksheet

Unit 1　Reading and Thinking

1. Figure out the painters of each painting and find some evidence from the text to support your ideas.

In my opinion, _____ is the painter of _____. The reasons are as follows.

First, _____. Additionally / Besides this / What's more, _____
_____

Thus, I'm convinced that _____ is the painter of _____.

2. Suppose you are a volunteer at a Western painting exhibition. Please introduce one of the four paintings (page 3, Student Book) to visitors from at least three aspects.

Ladies and gentlemen, I'm glad to have this opportunity to introduce to you the painting (the name of the painting) by (the name of the painter) .

_____

_____

Thank you for your attention. I hope you will all enjoy this fine piece of art.

| (1) period, the reasons for the development of Western painting in the period |
| (2) theme　　(3) subject　　(4) technique |
| (5) painter, the importance of the painter, other influential painters in the same period |

development, begin, change, gradually replace, breakthrough, build upon, innovation, increasingly shift from... to ..., emerge

3. Assignment: (1) Please finish Activity 3 (page 3, Student Book).

　　　　　　　(2) Choose one of the paintings and write down your explanation logically.

In my opinion, the first/second/third/fourth painting belongs to ... The reasons are as follows.

First, in subject matter, ... Besides, as for how it was painted, ... Finally, the purpose of it is to / its aim is to / it attempts to / it seeks to ...

Thus, I'm convinced that ...

_____
_____
_____

四、教学反思

本节课各教学目标达成情况较好。从学生的表现来看，他们已经较充分地把握和理解四个历史时期西方绘画艺术的发展概况。真实的活动场景、教师提供的语言支架，以及循序渐进的活动设计，都极大地调动了学生参与的积极性。在某些环节，学生甚至有超出教师预期的精彩表现，如分享自己对绘画艺术的背景知识、表达自己的主观感受，输出内容恰当、丰富且有深度。

本节课存在一些不足之处。第一，学生在梳理推动西方绘画艺术发展的重要因素时，仅仅分析了文本的表层信息。教师没有引导学生进一步挖掘文本深层信息，展开深层次阅读和思考。第二，在最后环节，学生汇报完成后，教师仅对学生的优点进行了肯定，未能针对其内容或语言，尤其是在运用表达"变化"的语言方面提出改进建议，错失了指导学生进一步提升语言表达能力的机会。教师应进一步增强课堂反馈的精准性和指导性。

第三节 提高版教学案例

教学内容安排：第一课时帮助学生整体理解文本，梳理文本基本信息，探究西方绘画艺术的发展历程；第二课时引导学生深入阅读文本，探究推动西方绘画艺术发展的重要因素，思考作者的写作手法和目的，探讨艺术的本质和价值。

第一课时

一、课时目标

1. 通过浏览图片和标题，进入单元主题语境，激活核心话题词汇，为梳理文本信息构建思维框架。

2. 通过略读和扫读，识别文本特征，快速定位关键词，厘清文本结构，识别作者的写作意图。

3. 通过细读，关注词句的表意功能、句子之间以及段落之间的衔接，整体感知西方绘画艺术的发展历程，梳理不同时期西方绘画艺术的特征。

4. 通过在情境中辨别和赏析绘画作品，深入探究西方绘画艺术的发展历程，加深对文本主题意义的理解。

二、设计思路

本节课以促进文本信息的获取、梳理、整合和运用为指向展开。教师首先通过情境设计，让学生辨别和赏析四幅创作于不同时期的绘画作品，激发学生对相关话题的兴趣；接着引导学生浏览标题，预测文本内容，形成阅读期待。在文本阅读环节，教师首先让学生通过快速阅读全文，厘清文本结构；接着让学生细读第一段，思考作者的写作意图和行文思路；之后让学生阅读第二至第八段，找出体现不同时期西方绘画艺术"变化"的句子，整体感知其发展历程；然后引导学生再读文本，找出不同时期西方绘画艺术的特征，从绘画艺术的主题、题材和技巧三个方面对这些特征进行纵向梳理；最后引导学生重回导入部分的情境，辨别和赏析绘画作品，学以致用。

三、教学过程

Activity 1: Viewing and talking about Western paintings and the title

本活动旨在落实课时目标1。

1. Talk about the four paintings.

Q1: Were these paintings painted in the same period of time?

Q2: How did you know?

2. Talk about the title of the text.

Q1: What are the key words in the title?

Q2: What do you think of when you read the word "history"?

Q3: What pops into your mind when you think of Western painting?

【设计意图】借助图片，激活学生的背景知识，激发学生的学习兴趣，同时为后面的活动，即要求学生辨别和赏析绘画作品做好准备；引导学生通过标题预测文本内容，激活核心话题词汇，为后面的文本信息梳理构建思维框架，并形成阅读期待。

【核心素养提升点】提升学生感知主题和预测话题的能力；培养学生的发散性思维能力。

Activity 2: Skimming and discovering the structure of the text

本活动旨在落实课时目标2。

Read and identify the structure of the text.

Q1: How many parts are there in the text?

Q2: What is the function of Paragraph 1?

Q3: What is the topic of the text?

【设计意图】引导学生通过快速阅读文本，识别文本特征，厘清文本结构，了解文本的基本内容和作者的写作意图。

【核心素养提升点】提升学生识别信息之间主次关系的能力。

Activity 3: Reading and exploring the development of Western painting

本活动旨在落实课时目标3。

1. Read the text and find the sentences showing the changes in the development of Western painting.

Q: What sentences in the text show the changes in the development of Western painting over the four periods?

T: You may refer to "Identify change" on page 2 of the Student Book to help you.

【设计意图】引导学生进行自主阅读，整体感知西方绘画艺术的发展历程，避免碎片化理解文本内容；引导学生运用阅读策略，构建核心话题词汇链，实现对语言的迁移和运用。

【核心素养提升点】提升学生的语言感知能力；提升学生的分析判断能力。

2. Read the text again and find detailed information about the changes over the four periods.

- The Middle Ages

Q1: How did Western painting change in this period?

Q2: In what aspect did Western painting change?

- The Renaissance

Q1: How did Western painting change in this period?

Q2: In what aspect did Western painting change?

- Impressionism

Q1: Who are mentioned in this period?

Q2: Why are they mentioned?

- Modern Art

Q1: What did subsequent artists do next?

Q2: What changes did they make?

Q3: What did they have in common?

> 【设计意图】引导学生自主梳理不同时期西方绘画艺术的特征，并从绘画艺术的主题、题材和技巧三个方面对这些特征进行纵向梳理，深入理解西方绘画艺术发展的相关知识。
>
> 【核心素养提升点】提升学生分析和整合信息的能力。

Activity 4: Identifying Western paintings

本活动旨在落实课时目标4。

Match the labels with the four paintings from different periods.

T: Imagine you are a volunteer in a famous gallery. You are asked to introduce four paintings to visitors. However, the paintings' labels are mixed up. Try to match the paintings with the correct labels. Explain your choices in terms of theme, subject, and technique.

> 【设计意图】通过创设真实情境，引导学生活用文本信息和语言知识，进行语段建构和意义表达，加深对文本主题意义的理解。
>
> 【核心素养提升点】培养学生的知识迁移和创新能力；提升学生的综合语言运用能力。

Assignment

Review the text and retell how Western painting developed over the four periods.

> 【设计意图】引导学生回顾文本，自主完善并强化对文本信息的整体认知，构建清晰的思维框架，进一步内化并创造性运用文本语言。
>
> 【核心素养提升点】提升学生的语言表达能力；培养学生的自主学习能力。

四、教学反思

本节课教学目标达成情况较好。为了减少文本话题"绘画艺术"与学生的距离感，在进入文本阅读环节之前，教师引导学生从视觉上感知绘画作品、激活核心话题词汇，为梳理文本信息构建思维框架。在阅读环节，教师提示学生运用阅读策略，整体感知西方绘画艺术的发展历程，避免碎片化理解文本，并构建核心话题词汇链。此外，教师给予学生充分的自主阅读时间，并在每次阅读前都给出清晰的阅读任务。这种方式有利于学生充分梳理文本信息，更好地把握文本主题意义。

本节课存在一些不足之处。由于文本对四个时期西方绘画艺术的叙述方式各不相同，因此教师很难设计一个统领全篇的问题来指导学生进行第二轮无干扰自主阅读，只能让学生开展分段阅读。在这种情况下，教师提出的引导性问题较多，对学生的阅读节奏具有一定的干扰性。同时，部分设问引导不够到位，学生的回答只停留在对表层信息的理解上。例如，在分析印象派时期的绘画艺术特征时，教师提出的两个问题"Who are mentioned?"和"Why are they mentioned?"旨在引导学生理解印象派的两种不同绘画风格，但在实际教学中，学生只是通过画家名字找到文本原句，没有分类梳理信息。教师应在学生阅读前提问"What is special about them?"并引导学生找到承上启下的句子，从而对比两种绘画风格的不同。此外，在活动4的汇报环节，学生的语言表达不够完整，句式较单一，段落组织不够严谨。教师可在活动中给学生提供必要的语言支架，帮助学生更流畅地表达。

第二课时

一、课时目标

1. 再读文本，探究和梳理推动西方绘画艺术发展的重要因素，关注有关因果关系的语言表达，体会文本的行文逻辑。
2. 赏析文本，识别文本的语言特征，分析作者的写作手法，提升语言赏析能力。
3. 回溯作者的写作目的，结合单元主题，阐释对艺术的理解。

二、设计思路

本节课基于第一课时学生已掌握的西方绘画艺术发展的相关知识，重点设计描述、评价、创新类学习活动，在内容（What）方面引导学生深入探究推动西方绘画艺术发展的重要因素，在语言（How）方面指导学生分析文本的语言特征和作者的写作手法，在思维（Why）方面引导学生通过回溯作者的写作目的，阐释对艺术的理解。教师首先让学生复述西方绘画艺术发展历程，完善对话题的认知；接着让学生阅读文本，梳理推动西方绘画艺术发展的重要因素，引导学生基于已有认知进一步思考助推艺术发展的深层动力；然后让学生回顾文本，分析作者的写作手法；最后引导学生结合单元话题，赏析有关艺术的名言，创造自己的佳句，阐释对艺术的理解。本节课各类活动综合性较强，对学生的思维能力要求较高，教师应通过示范呈现、互助合作等方式提供活动支架，提升学生的学习效果。

三、教学过程

Activity 1: Retelling the development of Western painting

本活动为实现课时目标1做铺垫。

Retell the development of Western painting over the four periods.

【设计意图】引导学生通过复述西方绘画艺术发展历程，回顾文本内容和话题语言，完善认知，并自然过渡到下一个活动环节。

【核心素养提升点】提高学生整合文本信息、传递文本要义的能力。

Activity 2: Reading and exploring the causes of the development of Western painting

本活动旨在落实课时目标1。

1. Read the text again and think about the causes of the development of Western painting.

Q1: What caused the development of Western painting over the four periods?

Q2: What does the phrase "as a result" imply?

Q3: What does "built upon" tell you?

Q4: Why does the writer say "from this"?

Q5: Why did the artists ask "What do we do next?"?

2. Think about some other causes of the development of Western painting.

T: Besides what is mentioned in the text, there must be some other causes. Please work in groups and share your opinions on some possible other causes.

> 【设计意图】引导学生通过自主阅读和思考教师提出的问题，关注文本中有关因果关系的语言表达，探讨推动西方绘画艺术发展的重要因素，并探究文本没有提到的其他因素，丰富相关认知，加深对话题的理解。
>
> 【核心素养提升点】培养学生的逻辑思维能力；提升学生表述因果关系的能力。

Activity 3: Reading and determining the writing skills

本活动旨在落实课时目标2。

Read to figure out the writing skills used in the text.

Q1: Do you think the text is well written?

Q2: What writing skills are used to make the text impressive?

> 【设计意图】引导学生赏析文本，领会作者如何遣词造句、谋篇布局，分析其所采用的设问、举例、对比等多种写作手法。
>
> 【核心素养提升点】提升学生的语言赏析能力；强化学生的语篇意识。

Activity 4: Focusing on the understanding of the theme "art"

本活动旨在落实课时目标3。

1. Explore the value of art.

T: The writer has applied multiple writing skills to make the language impressive, and you may also find the writer has an interesting way of beginning and ending the text.

Q: What's your understanding of art?

2. Appreciate some quotes by famous artists and create new sayings about art.

Q: What do you think of these quotes?

T: Refer to these quotes and create your own saying about art. While presenting your saying, try to refer to some information from the text to illustrate it.

【设计意图】引导学生通过关注文本首尾呼应的设问句,表达自己对艺术的理解;通过搭建支架,引导学生赏析关于艺术的名言,创造自己的佳句,结合文本内容阐释灵感的来源。

【核心素养提升点】提升学生的艺术素养;培养学生的文化意识。

Assignment

Your friend George is going to give a speech about Western art but needs some help. Write a letter to him to explain your understanding of Western art. Try to use information and language from the text.

【设计意图】引导学生结合文本内容、语言与写作手法,给朋友写一封信,表达自己对艺术的理解,实现语言和知识的迁移和运用,提升书面表达能力。

【核心素养提升点】培养学生严谨思考、准确表达的思维习惯;提升学生的综合素养。

The teacher's version:

Dear George,

I am more than delighted to share with you my understanding of Western art.

It is hard to define Western art in a short passage. However, you can surely gain a profounder perception of it by looking at the development of Western painting, which has gone through four periods—the Middle Ages, the Renaissance, Impressionism, and Modern Art.

From my perspective, art is not only a mirror of society but also the bridge between human souls and the world. Take the Renaissance for instance; this period of time has produced some of the greatest art in the history of Europe. The liberation of people's thoughts and values, the development of painting techniques, and the inheritance of painting concepts from former artists all played a decisive role. After the Renaissance, the Industrial Revolution took place and technology developed rapidly. All these revolutionary changes were then reflected in art.

The development of art is sure to continue forever. I hope my knowledge of Western painting has helped in your understanding.

Yours,
Li Ming

四、教学反思

本节课总体上较好地实现了教学目标。学生参与度高,讨论热烈,思考有深度,发言时有精彩表现。为了保证教学效果,教师在设计活动时充分注意难易梯度和支架搭建,例如:在探究推动西方绘画艺术发展的重要因素时,遵循"从已知到未知"的原则;在赏析作者写作手法时,运用"先示范后自主"的策略;在通过关注文本首尾呼应来聚焦单元主题时,采用"边模仿边创造"的方式，逐步引导学生阐释自己对艺术的理解。

　　本节课存在一些不足之处。在学生自主阅读并梳理推动西方绘画艺术发展的重要因素之后，教师以四个时期为序逐一让学生锁定并核实信息，这个部分的处理较为生硬。教师可以不拘时序，让学生自由表达，这样更能打开学生的思路，在课堂上形成自由互动的氛围。由于时间紧张，教师在引导学生赏析作者写作手法时比较匆忙，没有给学生足够的时间来表达。同样，在最后学生阐释自己对艺术的理解这个环节，如果时间更充分，学生的表现应该会更好。

UNIT 2 HEALTHY LIFESTYLE
Reading and Thinking HABITS FOR A HEALTHY LIFESTYLE

第一节 文本解读

一、总体解读

本单元的主题是"健康的生活方式"。阅读文本"Habits for a Healthy Lifestyle"旨在帮助学生深刻认识坏习惯对健康生活的不良影响,并学会运用心理学中的习惯循环原理,正确剖析自身习惯,掌握改变坏习惯的科学方法,坚定养成良好习惯的信心,帮助自身和他人改变坏习惯、养成好习惯,从而培养积极的生活态度和健康的生活方式。

该文本是一篇问题解决型的说明性文本。文本结构清晰、完整。作者先提出问题,即人们在青少年时期容易形成不良生活习惯,再阐述习惯的内涵和运作机制,然后运用科学知识为有效解决问题提供行动指南。在文本内容的组织上,作者多次使用例子和引言进行说明,并充分利用段落末句承上启下的功能,巧妙安排重要信息的位置,提高文本内容的连贯性。作者的写作目的在于帮助青少年科学地改变不良的生活习惯,培养健康的生活方式。

全文共六段。第一段阐述了青少年时期的坏习惯会带来长久而严重的身心危害,提出了青少年应尽早学会识别坏习惯并作出恰当改变。第二段用亚里士多德的名言引出习惯、选择与生活方式三者之间的关系,阐明了习惯的特征——选择性、重复性和自发性。第三段利用现代心理学知识,揭示了习惯的运作机制,为后文分析如何改变坏习惯、培养好习惯提供了科学方法。第四段聚焦习惯循环原理的应用价值,举例说明如何运用习惯循环原理来改变不良习惯、养成健康生活习惯。第五段阐述了影响坏习惯改变过程的其他关键因素,包括时间、自律和持续的努力等等。第六段呼吁青少年为培养健康快乐的生活方式作出反思,并付诸行动。

在阅读中,教师可引导学生运用如下阅读策略:通过自主提问预测文本内容;通过快速阅读把握问题解决型文本的结构特征;锁定关键信息,概括段落大意;运用思维导图,复述文本结构与内容;结合生活中的例子,理解和分析不同习惯养成中的触发因素(cue)、惯常行为(routine)和回报(reward),正确认识和运用习惯循环原理;结合上下文语境进行语言学习;等等。

二、段落解读

表1：分段解读

The original text	Interpretation
HABITS FOR A HEALTHY LIFESTYLE	**What questions can be raised about the title?** (1) What is a lifestyle? (2) What kind of lifestyle is healthy? (3) What is a habit? (4) What habits will be focused on? (5) How are habits formed? (6) What's the relationship between habits and a healthy lifestyle? (7) What text type will it be?
As teenagers grow up, they become more independent and start making their own decisions. However, during this period, it can be easy for some of them to form bad habits. These bad habits, if left unchecked, could lead to more serious ones when they become adults. For example, some of them may become involved in tobacco or alcohol abuse, which can lead to physical and mental health problems. To prevent harmful habits like these from dominating a teenager's life is essential. They must learn to recognise bad habits early and make appropriate changes.	**1. What does the writer say happens as teenagers grow up?** They become more independent and start making their own decisions. **2. What problem do teenagers have as they grow up?** They are likely to form bad habits easily. **3. What harmful effects could appear if bad habits are left unchecked?** Things like tobacco or alcohol abuse can cause physical and mental health problems and dominate a teenager's life. **4. What does "dominating a teenager's life" mean?** It means greatly affecting their life in an unpleasant way. **5. Why does the writer give the examples of tobacco and alcohol abuse?** To explain and support the previous opinion that "if left unchecked", bad habits could become "more serious ones" in the long run. **6. What suggestion does the writer give to combat the problem?** Teenagers must learn to identify bad habits as soon as possible and act or think differently to solve the problem. **7. What's the function of the last sentence of the paragraph?** This sentence ends the paragraph on a positive note and introduces the following paragraphs. Paragraphs 2 and 3 are about learning to "recognise bad habits", while Paragraphs 4 and 5 are about making "appropriate changes".

续表

The original text	Interpretation
To change bad habits is never easy, even with many attempts. There is a famous saying based on the philosophy of Aristotle: "We are what we repeatedly do." In many ways, our lifestyle is the sum of choices we have made. We make a choice to do something, and then we repeat it over and over again. Soon that choice becomes automatic and forms a habit that is much harder to change. The good news is that we can change, if we understand how habits work.	**1. What is a habit?** According to the key words in this paragraph, "repeat", "choice", and "automatic", a habit is something that we choose to do repeatedly until it becomes automatic. **2. Why is it that, even after many attempts, we often fail to change bad habits?** Because habits, good or bad, are the choices we make that are repeated so many times that they become automatic. **3. What is meant by "We are what we repeatedly do."?** When we do something over and over again, it will gradually and naturally become part of our life, thus forming what we are. **4. Why does the writer cite the famous saying?** To introduce the topic—how habits are formed—and to support the following sentences. **5. What can be inferred from the word "soon"?** It is easy to form a bad habit. **6. According to the writer, is it possible to change bad habits? How?** Yes, as long as we understand how habits work and make appropriate changes. **7. What's the function of the last sentence?** It shows the writer's opinion on changing bad habits and meanwhile introduces the main idea of the next paragraph, making the connection between the paragraphs natural and coherent.
According to modern psychology, we must first learn about the "habit cycle", which works like this: • Firstly, there is a "cue", an action, event, or situation that acts as a signal to do something. • Secondly, there is a "routine", the regular action you take in response to the cue.	**1. What are the three stages of the habit cycle?** Cue, routine, and reward. **2. What causes us to start a habit?** The cue, which is an action, event, or situation serving as the "signal". **3. What makes us continue to form a habit?** The reward, which gives us a "good thing or feeling". **4. What difficulty may a teenager have when analysing a bad habit using the habit cycle?**

The original text	Interpretation
• Thirdly, there is the "reward", the good thing or feeling we get from the routine. 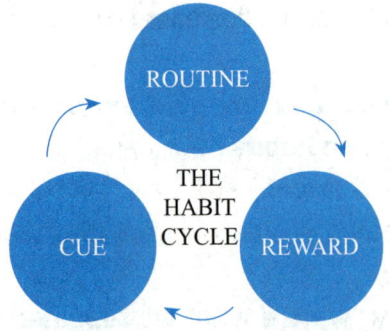 For example, when we feel unhappy (cue), we eat lots of unhealthy snacks (routine), which makes us feel happy (reward). The reward makes us much more likely to continue the cycle, and the bad habit of relying on unhealthy snacks is formed.	Perhaps figuring out the routine and reward correctly. **5. How does the writer help to explain the habit cycle?** By providing a definition, a diagram, and a specific example, making the abstract theory easier to understand. **6. What language is used to describe the habit cycle theory?** Key terms: cue, routine, reward Language used to describe the process of change: act as, take action, the good thing or feeling, form a bad habit, continue, rely on, in response to, signal, for example …
To facilitate a positive change in our bad habits, we must first examine our bad habit cycles and then try to adapt them. We can do this by combining the information from our habit cycles with our own positive ideas. For example, we could try to replace a negative routine with something more positive. So, when we feel unhappy again (cue), rather than eat snacks, we could listen to some of our favourite music instead (routine), which will make us feel relaxed (reward). Aside from changing bad habits, we can also use the habit cycle to create good habits. For example, when we come to an escalator (cue),	**1. What is this paragraph mainly about?** How to possibly cause a positive change in our bad habits. **2. To facilitate a positive change in our bad habits, what should be done? How is it explained?** We should adapt our bad habits into something better. The writer describes the stages of adapting habits and also gives examples. **3. How can we adapt bad habits?** By combining the information from our habit cycles with our own positive ideas. **4. How do we examine our bad habit cycles?** We find the cue, analyse the routine, and note the reward. **5. What are the differences between the two examples given in this paragraph?** The first example explains how to change from a negative routine to a positive one, while the second example explains how to replace a normal routine with a more positive one.

续表

The original text	Interpretation
our normal routine is to ride it, but we could change this routine into something more positive by taking the stairs instead.	**6. Why doesn't the writer mention the reward in the second example?** Because it is implied that the reader knows the reward is to feel happier about having a healthier lifestyle.
Many of us try to change bad habits quickly, and if we are not successful straight away, we often become pessimistic and give up. In fact, the most successful way to change is not suddenly, but over a period of time. As the Chinese philosopher Laozi wrote, "A journey of a thousand miles begins with a single step." One step seems small, but it is essential. To reach the goal of change, a person must show some discipline and repeatedly take many small steps. After all, it is not easy to break bad habits.	**1. What is this paragraph mainly about?** It is about what it takes to successfully change bad habits. **2. What makes us feel pessimistic and give up when we want to change bad habits?** Failing to change bad habits right away. **3. Why does the writer cite Laozi?** To highlight the importance of each and every small step in accomplishing something big and tough. **4. What is most likely to be the first single step in breaking bad habits?** The willingness and eagerness to live a healthy life. **5. To reach the goal of change, what else is needed?** Discipline and repeated small steps. **6. What is a person of "discipline" like?** A person of discipline possesses the ability to follow certain rules or standards and control their behaviour or the way they live, work, etc. **7. Besides knowledge, what else is needed to change bad habits?** Changing bad habits takes time, willingness, eagerness, discipline, and continuous efforts. **8. Why is "after all" used at the beginning of the last sentence?** It emphasises the difficulty of changing a bad habit.
For young people, there is plenty of time to change bad habits. However, there is no "magic pill" or delete button that will help you; you have to think about your bad habits and decide on some changes.	**1. What message does the writer want to convey?** Don't expect changing bad habits to be easy or quick. You must take action to change your bad habits to good ones, or you will never be able to build a happy and healthy life.

续表

The original text	Interpretation
You have the power to build a happy and healthy life full of good habits!	**2. What is meant by "magic pill" and "delete button"?** These two expressions are metaphors for "an instant way of stopping a bad habit". **3. What can be learnt from the last sentence of this paragraph?** The writer is trying to inspire young people to develop a belief that they can do something, e.g. develop good habits.

表2：跨段解读

Putting it all together
1. What is the text mainly about? The text is mainly about how to help teenagers recognise and change bad habits, thus living a healthy life. **2. How does the writer support his opinion?** The writer supports his opinion by giving definitions, a clear diagram, vivid examples, and convincing sayings. **3. How is the text organised?** Paragraph 1 states the writer's viewpoint—the necessity to learn to recognise bad habits early and make appropriate changes. Paragraphs 2 and 3 are mainly focused on how to recognise and understand habits. Paragraphs 4 and 5 are mainly about how to make appropriate changes. Paragraph 6 is intended to appeal to young people to change their bad habits and live a happy and healthy life. **4. What's the writing purpose?** The text is written to help young people identify, understand, and analyse their problems. It also provides them with a possible solution and strengthens their resolve to change bad habits. **5. In what ways do you think the habit cycle can help you to break a bad habit?** The habit cycle helps us identify and analyse the problems we have, and indicates clearly what we need to consider in order to solve the problems. **6. What power does the text give you to change bad habits?** The power of knowledge. Knowing about the habit cycle allows me to analyse my habits and make changes over time through willingness, discipline, continuous efforts, and repeated actions. It also empowers me to want to tackle my bad habits.

三、综合解读

综合上述分析，我们对文本进行教学设计时，应着重考量以下两个方面。

1. 语言学习

阅读文本所属单元话题为"健康的生活方式"（Healthy Lifestyle）。围绕该话题，文本教学可关注如下词汇：physical and mental health、habit、appropriate、reward、alcohol、tobacco、abuse、facilitate、examine、negative、repeatedly、automatic、discipline、power、dominate、rely on 等。此外，教师还可引导学生重点关注如下词汇：never、even、soon、aside from、after all 等，分析它们在句子衔接以及情感态度表达上的重要作用。在语篇知识方面，教师可引导学生关注作者的写作手法，如举例和引用等，以及段落末句在语篇连贯性中所起的关键作用。值得注意的是，教师在帮助学生学习语言时，应尽可能融合文本内容的学习及思维的培养，例如：引导学生利用上下文语境推测 adapt、facilitate 等词的含义；让学生通过对比，理解 soon、never、even 等词的作用；引导学生在分析不同习惯的运作机制中准确理解 reward、rely on、examine 等词汇的意思；帮助学生通过思考抽象词汇的具体行为表现，学习 dominate、discipline 等生词；等等。

2. 思维培养

第一，在分段阅读时，教师应提示学生注意分析句与句之间的逻辑关系，定位主题句，理解第一至第四段末句的"启下"作用。第二，教师要引导学生在"健康的生活方式"这一语境中解读"习惯"一词的含义。教师可引导学生利用思维导图梳理文本结构，总结坏习惯的危害，探究习惯形成的原因，运用习惯循环原理，理解问题和解决问题，进行自我剖析和自我完善，促进多元思维能力的发展。第三，教师应提示学生关注文本的叙述方式。叙述视角从第三人称到第一人称再到第二人称的转换，帮助实现了"客观分析""引发读者'对号入座'思考""增强号召力"的表意效果。

第二节　通用版教学案例

教学内容安排：第一课时引导学生通过整体阅读，提炼作者对习惯形成和改变的观点，然后聚焦第二至第四段，归纳习惯的三大特征和运作机制，并运用习惯循环原理剖析自身和他人身上的不良习惯，总结改变坏习惯的科学方法；第二课时引导学生聚焦第五和第六段，提炼影响坏习惯改变过程的其他关键因素，然后利用思维导图，梳理文本内容和结构，并综合运用所学内容和语言，解决实际问题。

第一课时

一、课时目标

1. 通过整体阅读，提炼作者对习惯形成和改变的观点，明确文本主线，提高文本分析能力。

2. 通过提炼关键词和下定义，概括习惯的三大特征——选择性、重复性和自发性，形成对习惯的科学认识。

3. 通过小组合作和情境创设，准确理解习惯循环原理中的触发因素、惯常行为和回报，合理分析青少年常见坏习惯的运作机制，总结改变坏习惯的科学方法。

4. 运用习惯循环原理剖析自己最想改变的坏习惯，提出可行的解决办法，提升自我分析和解决问题的能力。

二、设计思路

本节课围绕"讨论问题—提炼观点—分析原因—思考办法"四个环节展开。首先，教师利用单元开篇页主题图引出话题——习惯与生活方式，引导学生探讨当前青少年中常见的好习惯和坏习惯，激活话题背景知识。学生结合自身经历，针对坏习惯形成和改变的难易程度，发表看法。接着，教师引导学生快速阅读全文，明确作者对于改变坏习惯的态度。随后，教师引导学生通过分段阅读，进一步理解文本内容。学生通过细读第二段，梳理并概括习惯的概念，明晰习惯的三大特征；通过细读第三段，同时配合小组合作和情境活动，深入理解坏习惯形成的过程；通过细读第四段，理解如何运用习惯循环原理分析并改变坏习惯，并得出结论：改变坏习惯的关键在于改变习惯循环中的惯常行为。最后，教师布置任务，引导学生运用习惯循环原理剖析自己的坏习惯，并思考如何科学地改变它们。

三、教学过程

Activity 1: Talking about lifestyles and habits

本活动为实现课时目标1做铺垫。

1. Talk about the pictures on page 13 of the Student Book.

Q1: How do you think the people feel in the pictures?

Q2: What do you think of their lifestyle?

Q3: Do you think they all have a healthy lifestyle?

T: It seems not all happy lifestyles are healthy.

Q4: Is your lifestyle healthy or not?

2. Talk about bad habits.

Q1: Do you think it is easy to form bad habits?

Q2: Do you think it is easy to change bad habits?

【设计意图】引导学生浏览和讨论开篇页主题图，引出话题；通过让学生讨论习惯对生活方式的影响，引导他们正确看待快乐与健康之间的辩证关系，激活学生的话题背景知识，使他们形成阅读期待。

【核心素养提升点】帮助学生学会观察多模态语篇中的图片并理解其传递的意义；提升学生思考事物之间辩证关系的能力。

Activity 2: Reading to figure out the writer's attitude

本活动旨在落实课时目标1。

Read the whole text and figure out the writer's attitude.

Q1: Is it easy for teenagers to form and change bad habits? Please underline the key information in the text.

Q2: Can the words "never" and "even" be left out of the first sentence? Why?

> To change bad habits is never easy, even with many attempts . There is a famous saying based on the philosophy of Aristotle: "We are what we repeatedly do." In many ways, our lifestyle is the sum of choices we have made. We make a choice to do something, and then we repeat it over and over again. Soon that choice becomes automatic and forms a habit that is much harder to change. The good news is that we can change, if we understand how habits work.

Q3: Is it impossible to change bad habits? Why?

【设计意图】引导学生通过整体阅读，提炼作者的观点——坏习惯虽难改变，但我们通过科学方法还是能够成功改变它们的；引导学生感受never、even在情感态度表达上的作用。

【核心素养提升点】培养学生提取文本主要观点的能力；提升学生理解文本要义的能力。

Activity 3: Reading to work out what a habit is

本活动旨在落实课时目标2。

Read Paragraph 2 to work out what a habit is.

Q1: What are habits? Underline the key words in the text.

(choice, repeat, automatic)

Q2: Can you define "habit" in your own words?

(Habits are what we choose to do repeatedly and automatically.)

> 【设计意图】引导学生提取关键词,理解习惯一词的核心内涵,概括习惯的三大特征,并通过下定义,检测自己对习惯一词的理解。该活动同时融入repeatedly、automatic等话题词汇的学习,在一定程度上体现了内容、语言和思维的融合。
>
> 【核心素养提升点】提升学生的文本理解能力;培养学生的语言运用能力。

Activity 4: Reading to find out about how habits work

本活动旨在落实课时目标3。

1. Read Paragraph 3 to understand the three stages of the habit cycle.

Q1: How many stages are there in the habit cycle? What are they?

Q2: Could you read this sentence carefully and figure out the stages?

When we feel unhappy (   ), we eat lots of unhealthy snacks (   ), which makes us feel happy (   ).

Q3: What makes you think so?

(cue—the signal; routine—the regular action; reward—the good thing or feeling)

2. Decide whether the cycles below are reasonable habit cycles.

Q: Are the following cycles habit cycles? Work in groups and state your reasons.

> 【设计意图】步骤1帮助学生利用定义、图表和例子理解习惯循环原理,为正确分析习惯的运作机制做好准备。步骤2通过小组活动,让学生分析所给例子的合理性,检测学生是否准确理解习惯循环原理,提升学生的批判性思维能力。
>
> 【核心素养提升点】帮助学生领悟多模态语篇的表意功能;提升学生的逻辑思维能力和批判性思维能力。

Activity 5: Reading to summarise how to change bad habits

本活动旨在落实课时目标3。

Read Paragraph 4 to find out how to change bad habits with the habit cycle.

Q1: How can we change bad habits with the habit cycle?

Q2: What does "adapt" mean?

(It means "change", that is, to combine "the information from our habit cycles with our own positive ideas".)

Q3: Which stage does "the information" refer to? How did you know?

(It possibly refers to the routine. If you change the routine, you can change the bad habit.)

> 【设计意图】引导学生通过上下文语境，推断adapt的含义以及the information所指代的内容，明确改变坏习惯的关键在于改变惯常行为，进而提炼改变坏习惯的科学方法。
>
> 【核心素养提升点】提升学生在语境中准确理解关键字词的能力；提升学生的阅读理解能力；培养学生的推断能力。

Activity 6: Reflecting on your own bad habits

本活动旨在落实课时目标4。

Choose a habit you want to change but have failed to change. Then, using what you've learnt, try to understand, analyse, and break it.

> 【设计意图】引导学生运用习惯循环原理正确剖析自己的坏习惯，分析坏习惯的形成过程及运作机制，并根据所学方法，提出相应的解决办法。
>
> 【核心素养提升点】培养学生综合运用所学反思自我的能力；提升学生解决实际问题的能力。

Assignment

Do you have a habit you want to change but have failed to change? Why did you fail? After reading the text, please write about your bad habit. Analyse your habit and come up with an idea to break it.

The following may help you.

Structure	Language
Introduce the habit	abuse, be involved in
Explain the reasons	if left unchecked, lead to, dominate one's life, lifestyle, never easy, even with many attempts
Analyse the habit	automatic, modern psychology, diagram, the habit cycle, work like this, signal, continue the cycle, rely on
Put forward solutions	facilitate, examine, adapt, combine ... with ..., change ... into ...

> 【设计意图】引导学生根据实际情况，用书面表达的方式，反思自身最想改变却未成功改变的习惯，利用习惯循环原理进行恰当分析并提出解决方法。
> 【核心素养提升点】提升学生的综合语言运用能力；提升学生解决实际问题的能力。

The teacher's version:

I've **been** constantly **involved in** playing phone games with my friends for about one year. My homework has suffered as a result, and I'm sometimes tired at school. I've made **many attempts** to stop but always failed. Playing games is like tobacco **abuse**—it's not easy to stop. However, **if left** unchanged, my habit could **lead to** serious problems. I feel it is already beginning to **dominate** my life. Now that I know about **the habit cycle**, I can start to analyse and change my habit. As the **diagram** shows, after dinner (cue), I usually play phone games (routine), which makes me happy and excited (reward). The reward makes me **continue the cycle** and not want to stop.

To **facilitate** a positive change, I can try to **adapt** my habit cycle a little. For example, after dinner, I could read books instead of playing games. If I **change the routine** to something else I like, like reading books, I might have a chance of breaking my habit. Besides, I could still play at the weekend after I finish my homework properly.

四、教学反思

本节课教学主线清晰，整个教学过程从整体到局部，从浅层理解到深度学习，重点关注学生逻辑思维能力和批判性思维能力的培养，顺利实现了四个预设的课时目标。在最后，教师通过引导学生运用习惯循环原理剖析自己最想改变的不良习惯并尝试提出解决办法，聚焦了学生的真实问题，帮助学生从内容和语言角度实现综合输出，体现了活动的情境性、综合性和实践性。为了促进学生主动学习，教师设置了不同层次的师生互动和生生互动环节，例如：小组组员相互合作，利用习惯循环原理分析所给的三个例子是否合理。这个环节有效锻炼了学生的口头表达能力和批判性思维能力。此外，教师运用不同的方式融入语言学习，例如：引导学生通过对比，理解never、even两词在情感态度表达上的作用；引导学生通过上下文语境推测adapt的含义；等等。

本节课存在一些需要改进的地方。首先，虽然第一和第二个目标达成度较高，但教师设计的教学活动多以师生一问一答的形式进行，学生缺乏主动学习的机会。其次，教师虽然在最后一个环节呈现了与话题相关的语言，但没有让学生自主梳理这些语言。学生错过了主动创建单元话题词汇库的机会。最后，对于部分学生来说，该文本难度较大，专业术语较多，这在一定程度上增加了他们的阅读困难。教师应在语言上做更多的铺垫，以更好地帮助学生分析和理解文本。

第二课时

一、课时目标

1. 概括影响坏习惯改变过程的其他关键因素，主要包括时间、自律和"千里之行、始于足下"的精神，深刻认识坏习惯改变过程中非智力因素的重要作用。

2. 利用个性化思维导图，复述文本内容和结构，提升文本分析能力和逻辑思维能力。

3. 探讨power一词的内涵，表达对改变不良习惯、建立健康生活方式的信心和决心，完善改变坏习惯的具体措施。

二、设计思路

在本节课的学习中，教师首先引导学生通过分享自身不良习惯的形成过程和改变方法，回顾第一课时的重点内容和话题语言；接着通过提问，启发学生思考"有了习惯循环原理，改变坏习惯是否就能立竿见影？"，从而导入第二课时的学习；之后引导学生聚焦第五段，总结影响坏习惯改变过程的非智力因素，学习discipline、essential等词，同时理解文本中引用的老子名言；然后引导学生小组合作，根据文本内容和结构绘制和展示个性化的思维导图，并在教师的指导下总结文本脉络，即"呈现问题—分析问题—解决问题—启发鼓励"，领悟改变坏习惯的必要性、艰难性和可行性，表达对建立健康生活方式的信心和决心；最后布置作业，让学生撰写演讲稿，实现对文本内容和语言的迁移运用。

三、教学过程

Activity 1: Checking the assignment and introducing the lesson

本活动为实现课时目标1做铺垫。

1. Share your assignment in groups, and then in front of class.

Q1: What habit have you analysed?

Q2: How would you use the habit cycle to help yourself?

2. Share your opinions on whether the habit cycle can help break bad habits quickly.

Q: Do you think the habit cycle can help break your bad habits quickly? Why?

T: So, besides the habit cycle, maybe we need something else. Please read Paragraph 5 and find the answer.

【设计意图】步骤1引导学生回顾第一课时的重点内容和话题语言，同时检测学生对第一课时内容的掌握和运用情况。步骤2通过提问，启发学生思考"有了习惯循环原理，改变坏习惯是否就能立竿见影？"，目的是提升学生的批判性思维能力，并导入第二课时的学习。

【核心素养提升点】提升学生运用词汇准确表达意义的能力；提升学生的批判性思维能力。

Activity 2: Reading to find the key factors in changing bad habits

本活动旨在落实课时目标1。

1. Read Paragraph 5 and summarise what else is needed to change bad habits.

Q: According to the writer, besides knowledge, what else is needed to change bad habits?

(Time, continuous efforts, discipline.)

2. Share your understanding of discipline.

Q1: Do you know the meaning of discipline?

T: Here's an example for you. I wanted to form the healthy habit of jogging every day. At first, I went jogging every day. But one day, when I was supposed to go jogging, I ended up watching TV on my sofa. Gradually, I stopped going jogging. **Am I a person of discipline**?

Q2: What does "discipline" mean?

(It refers to the ability to control your behaviour.)

> 【设计意图】步骤1引导学生提炼影响坏习惯改变过程的非智力因素。步骤2聚焦语言难点discipline，通过生动的例子将抽象名词具体化和情境化，帮助学生理解discipline所表达的含义，体现了内容、语言和情感态度三者之间的融合。
>
> 【核心素养提升点】提升学生的信息概括能力；培养学生在语境中理解词义的能力；提升学生描述和说明概念的能力。

Activity 3: Reading to draw a mind map of the whole text

本活动旨在落实课时目标2。

1. Read the whole text and draw a mind map.

Q: Can you draw a mind map of the whole text?

2. Summarise the text.

Q: How would you summarise the whole text?

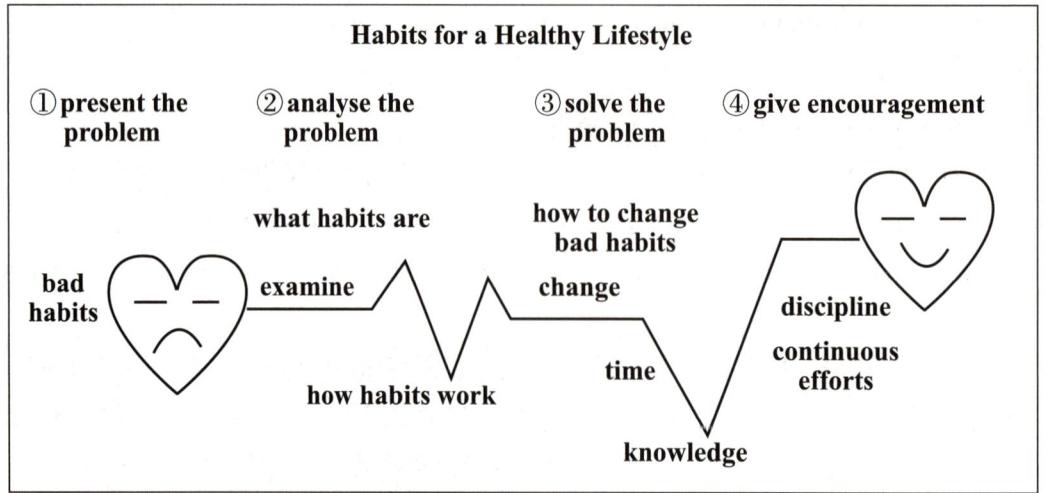

【设计意图】步骤1引导学生小组合作，绘制个性化的思维导图，达到自主梳理文本内容和结构的目的。步骤2引导学生进一步总结文本脉络，即"呈现问题—分析问题—解决问题—启发鼓励"，从而明确作者鼓励青少年建立健康生活方式的写作意图。

【核心素养提升点】提升学生自主梳理文本内容和结构的能力；培养学生的语篇意识；提升学生理解作者写作意图的能力。

Activity 4: Figuring out the possible meaning of "power" and expressing your strong determination to break bad habits

本活动旨在落实课时目标3。

Work in pairs and talk about what "power" possibly refers to.

Q: According to the writer, what power do young people have?

(The power to change, by learning about bad habits, and showing willingness, eagerness, discipline, and continuous efforts to live a healthy life.)

【设计意图】引导学生通过挖掘power一词的内涵，表达对改变不良习惯、建立健康生活方式的信心和决心。

【核心素养提升点】提升学生理解词汇内涵的能力；帮助学生树立正确的人生观和价值观。

Activity 5: Brainstorming for more ways to break bad habits

本活动旨在落实课时目标3。

Think of and share more ways to break bad habits.

Q1: Do you want to break your bad habits? Do you want to lead a healthy life?

Q2: How would you make a specific plan to break the bad habit you want to change?

【设计意图】引导学生进一步分析自我，结合影响坏习惯改变过程的非智力因素，针对自身特点，制订并完善改变坏习惯的具体措施。

【核心素养提升点】提升学生在真实情境中分析问题和解决问题的能力。

Assignment

The World Health Day is coming and you are invited to deliver an English speech named "Go Away, Mr Bad Habit". The following parts should be included:

- present the problems caused by your bad habit;
- share your ways to break it;
- share what you have gained after breaking it;
- give your proposal.

【设计意图】引导学生撰写演讲稿，分享自己改变坏习惯的例子，整体迁移运用所学文本内容、语言和结构，坚定改变坏习惯的决心，同时倡导更多同龄人改变自身不良习惯、建立健康的生活方式。

【核心素养提升点】提升学生的综合语言运用能力。

The teacher's version:

Dear friends,

 I'm Li Hua. I feel greatly honoured to deliver a speech to you all.

 Once, I was troubled by a bad habit—I used to stay up late chatting with my roommates when I felt stressed. After chatting, I did feel relaxed, but the next day, I felt too tired to do anything well, which meant my studies suffered a lot. I knew it was high time that I made some appropriate changes to prevent the harmful habit from dominating my life. However, to change a bad habit is never easy, even with many attempts. Not until I chose to do mindfulness training to relax myself did everything start to change for the better. For example, now when I am stressed out and tempted to chat with others, I sit in meditation, asking myself why I am so eager to chat, which makes me calm down and start to find other helpful ways to cope with my stress. Now I feel energetic again and have caught up with my classmates in study. What's more, I know myself better and I'm much happier.

 As the Chinese philosopher Laozi wrote, "A journey of a thousand miles begins with a single step." One step seems trivial, but it is essential. Act now and believe in yourself. You have the power to build a happy and healthy life that is full of good habits!

 Thank you, everyone!

四、教学反思

  本节课课堂节奏流畅，教学目标达成情况较好，突出了对学生批判性思维能力和问题解决能力的培养。在学生主动学习方面，教师不仅注重培养学生的小组合作意识和绘制个性化思维导图的能力，而且尝试引导学生借助文本内容，一步步深入认识自我、分析自我、完善自我，呼应了文本从第三人称到第一人称再到第二人称的写作视角。在语言学习方面，教师注重抽象概念的具象转换和表达，例如：针对语言难点discipline的处理，教师根据学生情况，利用生动的例子，将抽象名词具体化和情境化，这在一定程度上体现了内容、语言和情感态度三者之间的融合。

  本节课存在一些不足之处。首先，整节课教师引导的痕迹较重，从整体阅读到局部阅读的过程中，学生缺少主动提问的机会。其次，语言教学多次以关键字词理解为抓手，缺少更大语言单位的整理、操练、内化等活动。最后，在分享环节，教师应给予学生更多的分享时间，同时丰富评价方式，如增加学生自我评价和同伴互评等。

第三节 提高版教学案例

教学内容安排：第一课时引导学生通过整体阅读，提炼文本主旨大意，把握其主线和脉络，然后细读第一至第三段，明确青少年改变坏习惯的必要性，理解习惯循环原理并运用它剖析自身或同伴的坏习惯；第二课时引导学生细读第四至第六段，获知运用习惯循环原理改变坏习惯的基本策略，梳理改变坏习惯所需的主客观因素，提升解决问题的能力。

第一课时

一、课时目标

1. 通过整体阅读，提炼文本主旨大意，把握其主线和脉络。
2. 理解青少年要尽早改变坏习惯的必要性，归纳习惯的定义及形成过程，为改变坏习惯打下理论基础。
3. 通过猜测词义、解读关键句、下定义、挖掘段落间的关联、分析作者的写作手法等活动，培养逻辑思维能力。
4. 通过自主探究、作品互评，建立文本与生活的联系，进一步理解触发因素（cue）、惯常行为（routine）和回报（reward），培养自主学习能力和探究式学习能力。

二、设计思路

该文本不仅是一篇阅读文本，更是一份行动指南，对学生在现实生活中改变坏习惯有着实际的指导意义。由于文中关于习惯的定义、习惯循环原理的各阶段概念较为抽象，本节课的教学设计非常强调文本与学生生活的关联，注重让学生借助自身实际生活经历实现对文本的深入理解，并在理解的基础上进行各种语言实践活动，同时又借助文本中所学的知识来指导生活实践。

在本节课，教师首先从单元主题"健康的生活方式"入手，结合学生日常生活，引导学生意识到习惯和生活方式密切相关，激发学生进一步探究的兴趣；接着引导学生浏览标题，预测文本内容；随后让学生进行无干扰整体阅读，概括文本主旨大意，了解作者是如何展开论述的；然后让学生细读第一至第三段，通过猜测词义、解读关键句、下定义、挖掘段落间的关联、分析作者的写作手法等，深入理解文本；最后引导学生评价同伴作品是否合理，进一步检测学生对文本的理解。

三、教学过程

Activity 1: Talking about your daily life

本活动为实现课时目标 1 做铺垫。

1. **Look at the Opening Page and talk about healthy lifestyles.**

Q1: Do you want to have a healthy lifestyle?

Q2: Are you leading a healthy life?

Q3: What can prevent you from having a healthy lifestyle?

2. **Read the title of the text.**

Q: What can you get from the title?

【设计意图】围绕单元开篇页主题图和文本标题，通过师生间的自由对话，步步推进，引导学生思考是什么影响我们拥有健康的生活方式，从而主动发现习惯和健康生活之间的联系，预测文本内容，形成探究兴趣和阅读期待。

【核心素养提升点】培养学生探究问题本质的能力；提升学生的语言表达能力。

Activity 2: Reading to grasp basic and global comprehension

本活动旨在落实课时目标1。

Read for the main idea and the development of the text.

Q1: What is the main idea of the text?

Q2: How does the writer develop the text?

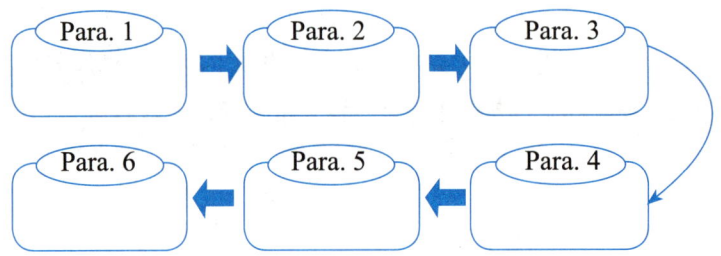

【设计意图】引导学生进行整体阅读，归纳文本主旨大意，梳理文本脉络，培养语篇意识。在此过程中，教师要减少对学生阅读过程的干扰，给予学生充分的阅读和思考时间。

【核心素养提升点】提升学生提炼文本主旨大意、把握文本脉络的能力；提升学生获取并理解文本要义的能力。

Activity 3: Reading to realise the necessity of changing bad habits

本活动旨在落实课时目标2和课时目标3。

Read Paragraph 1 to figure out why bad teenage habits should be changed.

Q1: Why should bad teenage habits be changed?

Q2: What suggestion does the writer give?

(They must learn to recognise bad habits early and make appropriate changes.)

【设计意图】借助相关问题链，引导学生逐步获取、梳理关键信息，从而理解青少年要尽早改变坏习惯的原因以及作者的有关建议，并学习相关话题单词dominate、tobacco、alcohol、abuse等。

【核心素养提升点】提升学生获取、梳理关键信息的能力。

Activity 4: Reading to learn how to recognise bad habits

本活动旨在落实课时目标2和课时目标3。

1. Read to judge whether a person has formed a bad habit.

Q: Did Li Hua form a bad habit? Read Paragraph 2 to find the answer.

> Li Ming noticed his brother, Li Hua, was playing games on his phone. Thinking Li Hua had become addicted to playing mobile games, he rushed to tell his parents.

2. Figure out the definition of a habit.

Q1: What is a habit?

Q2: According to the writer, is it easy to change bad habits?

Q3: Is it possible to change bad habits?

Q4: What is the function of the last sentence?

【设计意图】步骤1让学生在情境中理解抽象概念，促进学生自主阅读和思考。步骤2让学生用自己的语言定义"习惯"，通过归纳整合关键信息，建构新概念；引导学生明确坏习惯虽然难改但仍可改的事实，形成积极的态度；提示学生关注相关话题词汇以及第二段末句承上启下的功能。

【核心素养提升点】提升学生归纳整合关键信息的能力；培养学生建构新概念的能力；帮助学生树立语篇意识；提升学生的文本结构分析能力。

Activity 5: Reading to understand how habits work

本活动旨在落实课时目标3和课时目标4。

1. Examine the diagram and understand the habit cycle.

Q: What are the three stages of the habit cycle?

2. Read Paragraph 3 to find what other techniques are used to explain the habit cycle.

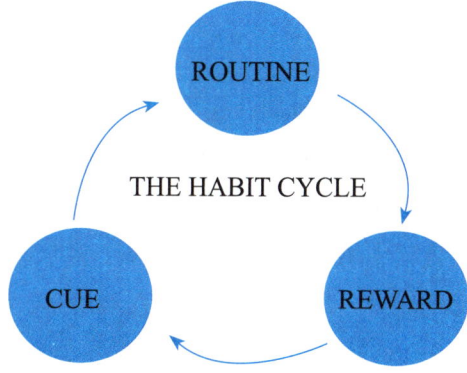

Besides using the diagram, the writer also explains the "habit cycle" by —
- giving definitions
- giving examples

3. Draw and analyse habit cycles.

T: In groups, choose a common bad teenage habit and analyse how it is formed. Then draw a habit cycle for the habit.

4. Share the habit cycles and discuss whether they are correct.

Q: Do you think their habit cycles are correct? Why?

Here are two habit cycles from some students and the teacher's response.

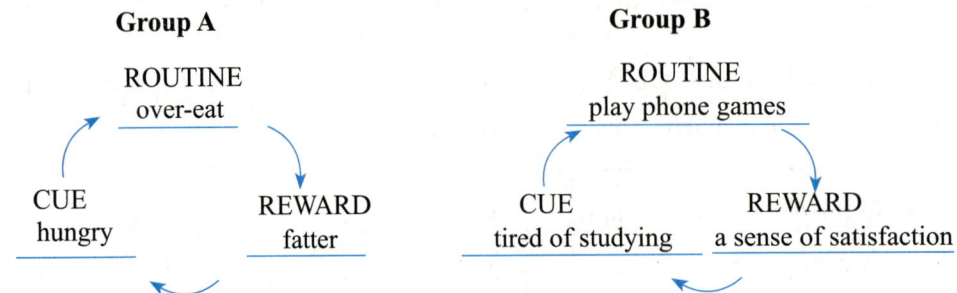

T: (Pointing at Group A's cycle) Do you think it is a habit cycle?

S1: (Shaking his head and referring to the definition of reward) The reward should be a good thing or feeling we get from the routine.

T: Yes, it is the reward that makes you repeat the behaviour. So we need to correct this habit cycle. (Asking the student who originally presented the habit cycle) How would you change your cycle?

S2: I will change the reward to "satisfied".

5. Make a summary.

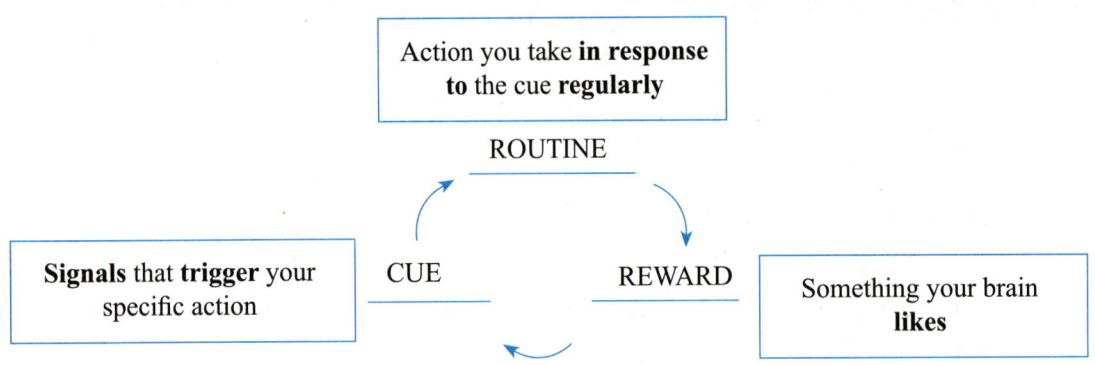

【设计意图】步骤1引导学生通过读图，直观了解习惯的运作机制，理解多模态语篇在建构意义中的作用。步骤2引导学生通过分析文中的定义和例子，明确作者的写作手法，初步理解习惯循环原理。步骤3引导学生通过联系生活实际，进一步理解触发因素（cue）、惯常行为（routine）和回报（reward），尝试利用所学解决生活中的实际问题。步骤4让学生通过解读部分同学的作品，开展同伴互评，提升批判性思维能力。步骤5引导学生总结所学，深入理解习惯循环原理。

【核心素养提升点】帮助学生理解多模态语篇的作用；培养学生将文本与实际生活相联系的能力；提升学生的批判性思维能力。

Assignment

Think of a bad habit that you want to change but have failed to change. State its bad effects and analyse how it is formed using the habit cycle.

【设计意图】作为阅读文本的课后复习和延伸，帮助学生正视和科学分析生活中真实存在的问题。

【核心素养提升点】提高学生认识和分析问题的能力；提升学生表达观点的能力；培养学生的逻辑思维能力。

The teacher's version:

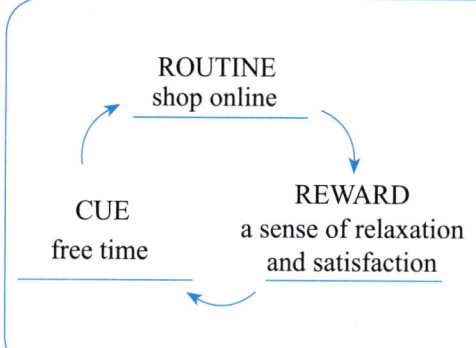

Every time I am free, I spend too much time surfing the Internet and purchasing whatever catches my eye, which brings me a sense of relaxation and satisfaction. Now my home is full of things I don't really need. My wallet is empty because my life is dominated by this terrible habit. I've reached the point where I can't fall asleep without first buying something.

四、教学反思

本节课教师从单元标题入手，设置问题链，引导学生明确习惯与生活方式密切相关，然后带领学生解读文本标题，明确文本阅读的入口和终极目标，为后面理解文本主题做了有效铺垫。接下来，教师让学生带着任务进行无干扰整体阅读，鼓励学生在遇到困难无法独自完成时进行互助合作。针对抽象概念的教学，教师巧妙地建立起文本与生活的联系，化抽象为具象，如归纳习惯的定义时，用李华是否真地沉迷游戏的例子，给原本枯燥的下定义环节增添了不少趣味。在阐述习惯循环的三个要素时，教师没有让学生直接阅读文中的定义，而是让学生关注多模态语篇的形式以及作者的写作手法，领会作者给出的定义和例子之间的关系，进而让学生画出自己的习惯循环图，并进行分析与阐述。然后，教师利用同伴互评环节，进一步检测学生对文本的理解。总体上，本节课较好地实现了教学目标，课堂氛围活跃，学生参与度高，表现符合预期。

本节课存在几点不足之处。第一，在学生整体阅读时，教师所布置的任务较难，学生需要更多的时间去理解和完成。因此，教师的讲解以及与学生的交流还应更充分些。例如，在提炼文本主旨大意时，教师可以多请几位学生发言。第二，教师的临场反应能力较为欠缺。教师虽然在前面解读文本标题环节处理得当，为学生接下来阅读文本做了有效铺垫，但在后面的活动中，特别是在提炼和呈现文本的主旨时表现得略有不足。第三，在学生细读第一段时，教师大量重复学生所陈述的答案，显得有点拖沓，不够简洁高效。第四，作业的内容可以再拓宽一些，给学生更大的自由度。

第二课时

一、课时目标

1. 通过课堂作业展示，恰当阐述改变坏习惯的原因，正确分析自身习惯的形成过程，巩固第一课时内容。

2. 通过细读文本，提炼习惯循环原理的应用价值，归纳影响坏习惯改变过程的其他关键因素，包括时间、自律和坚持等。

3. 通过猜测词义、解读关键句等，培养逻辑思维能力。

4. 通过个人探究、情境创设等活动，明确文本的目标读者群，总结改变坏习惯的科学方法，尝试解决自身或他人生活中的相关问题，培养健康的生活方式。

二、设计思路

本节课教师首先让学生展示第一课时作业，巩固内化第一课时所学，为进一步理解文本的内涵与意义做好铺垫；接着引导学生细读文本第四至第六段，提炼并理解习惯循环原理的应用价值，归纳影响坏习惯改变过程的其他关键因素，开展 facilitate、discipline、adapt 等词汇的语言学习；然后引导学生自主探究，探讨文本的目标读者群，通过图表总结两个课时所学；最后通过作业的设置，创设情境，引导学生利用所学知识解决自身或他人的相关问题，在实践中内化和运用所学，培养逻辑思维能力、探究式学习能力和创造性思维能力。

三、教学过程

Activity 1: Giving presentations

本活动旨在落实课时目标1。

Show your assignment and give a presentation.

【设计意图】通过作业展示和成果分享，帮助学生巩固内化第一课时所学，同时为第二课时的阅读做好铺垫。

【核心素养提升点】提升学生的综合语言运用能力；提升学生的逻辑思维能力和批判性思维能力。

Activity 2: Reading to apply the knowledge of the habit cycle

本活动旨在落实课时目标2和课时目标3。

1. Read Paragraph 4 carefully and find applications of the habit cycle.

Q1: How many applications of the habit cycle are given?

Q2: How did you find the answer? Are there any signal words?

Q3: What does the word "facilitate" mean?

Q4: How can we figure out a habit cycle?

(Find the cue, analyse the routine, and weigh the reward.)

Q5: How can we adapt bad habits?

2. Try to facilitate a positive change in a bad habit that you want to change but have failed to change.

【设计意图】通过设置问题链，由浅入深地引导学生理解习惯循环原理的两种应用价值，即改变坏习惯和养成好习惯；引导学生利用话语标记，如first、then、aside from，迅速检索信息，然后根据上下文猜测facilitate的词义；让学生再次利用第一课时的作业，针对想改但未改成的坏习惯，提出具体的建议。

【核心素养提升点】培养学生利用话语标记迅速检索信息的能力；提升学生根据上下文猜测词义的能力；培养学生利用所学知识解决生活中实际问题的能力；提升学生的语言表达能力；培养学生的逻辑思维能力。

Activity 3: Reading to find out other key factors in the process of changing bad habits

本活动旨在落实课时目标2和课时目标3。

1. Read Paragraph 5 and try to answer the question.

Q: What else is needed to change bad habits?

2. In groups, discuss how to use discipline to help change a bad habit.

Q: How can I use discipline to help change a bad habit?

> Every day, I spend too much time surfing the Internet and buying whatever **catches my eye**. Now my home is full of things I don't really need. My wallet is empty because my life is **dominated** by this terrible habit. I've **made many attempts to break the habit** but it has all been in vain because I'm not disciplined enough.

Here are some ideas to help change the bad habit:

- control the time on the Internet;
- write a reminder;
- control the money spent online.

【设计意图】步骤1引导学生分析和归纳影响坏习惯改变过程的其他关键因素，如行动、时间、自律和坚持等。步骤2通过具体的情境创设，将抽象概念具象化，引导学生思考如何靠自律改变坏习惯，同时复现dominate、make many attempts等重点单词和短语，帮助学生在学中用，在用中学，实现知识的内化和运用。

【核心素养提升点】提升学生的语言表达能力；培养学生的逻辑思维能力和创造性思维能力。

Activity 4: Reading to find out the intended readers and summarise the text

本活动旨在落实课时目标4。

1. Read Paragraph 6 aloud and think about the questions below.

Q1: Who does "you" refer to here?

(The word "you" here refers to young people.)

Q2: What power do you have to change bad habits after reading this text?

(Power of knowledge about the habit cycle, self-control/discipline, time, patience, repeated efforts, etc.)

2. Make a conclusion.

T: Today, we focused on learning about bad habits. Everyone's goal should be to live a healthy life. To reach this goal, we must have motivation and knowledge. First, we learnt some facts about habits, including what a habit is and how habits work. Then, we learnt about a habit-changing technique, which can help us to break bad habits. Using this information and technique can help us to solve many problems in our daily lives.

Habits for a Healthy Lifestyle

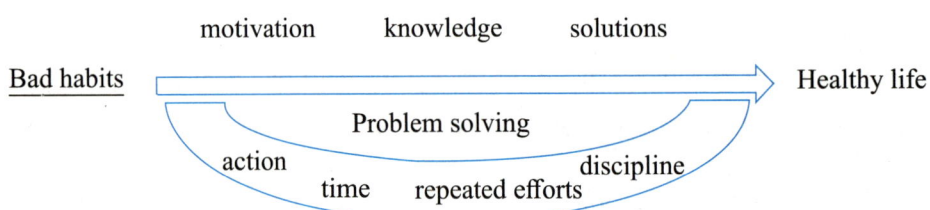

【设计意图】借助问题，引导学生明确文本的目标读者群，并通过挖掘power一词的内涵，总结两个课时的主要内容，提升阅读获得感和成就感。

【核心素养提升点】提升学生的语言表达能力；培养学生的逻辑思维能力；培养学生的探究式学习能力。

Assignment

Recently, Xiao Fan, a former top student, has spent more and more time on the Internet, which has worried his parents a lot. Today, they have taken him to your counselling office for help.

(1) Please analyse his behaviour using the habit cycle.

(2) Please give him some guidance to help him break his bad habit.

【设计意图】通过情境创设，引导学生在所学文本的基础上，筛选或添加适当信息，组织语言，利用所学知识解决自身或他人的相关问题。

【核心素养提升点】提升学生筛选和组织信息的能力；培养学生的创造性思维能力。

The teacher's version:

According to the description, we can conclude that Xiao Fan has developed the bad habit of using the Internet too much. The **cue** is probably the frustration and stress in his daily life. Growing pains together with academic pressures greatly frustrate Xiao Fan. So he turns to the Internet, the virtual world, where he can enjoy a sense of achievement

ROUTINE
depend on the Internet

CUE
frustration & stress

REWARD
a sense of achievement

and relaxation. Gradually, the Internet **dominates** his life. And he becomes more and more **pessimistic** in real life. Fear, a lack of self-confidence, and endless negative self-assessment, have all pulled him further away from reality. Just as the diagram shows.

To **facilitate** a positive change in the bad habit, I'd like to give Xiao Fan the following suggestions. Initially, he has to be fully aware of the negative effect the over-use of the Internet is having on his life. Then, it would be wise for him to figure out what he is good at and try his best to reinforce it to the fullest. As a result, he can enjoy a sense of achievement in his real life rather than in the virtual world. What's more, it is strongly recommended that Xiao Fan should keep his body and mind busy with something meaningful, such as doing more physical exercise or developing some new positive hobbies. Once he finds something more positive to do, he will be more likely to get rid of the bad habit.

四、教学反思

在本节课，教师引导学生关注话语标记，运用语篇知识迅速定位习惯循环原理的应用价值，并结合自己生活实际，主动发现改变坏习惯并非易事，进而梳理影响坏习惯改变过程的其他关键因素。面对抽象的概念理解和语言学习，教师再次巧设情境，用解决问题的方式，让学生表达自身对语言的理解，同时实现了对dominate、facilitate等生词和难词的复现。最后，教师巧抓power一词，引导学生回顾全文内容。总体上，本节课延续第一课时所铺设的线索，围绕"关注问题—确立目标—学习理论知识—寻找解决途径—归纳解决难题的其他要素"，循序渐进，步步展开。教师多次将文本内容与现实生活相联系，引导学生利用所学解决实际问题，并注重学生思维能力的培养。

本节课存在一些不足之处。首先，教师没有提前查看教学辅助设备，到上课前10分钟才发现设备故障，导致要改用其他更加费时的方式展示学生作业。同时，突发情况导致教师和学生都有些紧张，因此作业展示环节较为仓促。其次，在总结阶段，教师可将原活动改为让学生自主或分组绘制思维导图，给学生更多自主探究的机会。

UNIT 3 ENVIRONMENTAL PROTECTION
Reading and Thinking   CLIMATE CHANGE REQUIRES THE WORLD'S ATTENTION

第一节　文本解读

一、总体解读

　　本单元的主题是"环境保护"，主要探讨环境与人类生存以及社会发展之间的关系。阅读文本"Climate Change Requires the World's Attention"围绕"全球气候变暖"这个话题展开，目的在于引导学生认识相关环境问题，即人为因素造成的温室效应导致全球气候变暖，给生物生存乃至整个生态系统都带来了巨大影响。作者通过分析气候变化的成因和警示气候变化的后果，号召全人类提升环境保护意识，采取恰当行动，减少碳排放，共同应对气候变暖问题。

　　全文共五段，按照"现象—案例—原因—危害—对策"的顺序展开。第一段呈现气候现状：全球气候剧烈变化，地表温度逐年增高。第二段通过2013年北极熊饿死的案例，证明气候变暖给地球生态带来的负面影响。第三段介绍两种温室效应，探究全球气候变暖的原因。第四段揭示气候变暖的后果，即极端天气、自然灾害出现的频次增多，造成生命和财产的巨大损失。第五段亮出观点，呼应标题，并号召全球人民携起手来，采取相应对策，减少碳排放。

　　在阅读策略方面，教师可引导学生通过"看"图推测文本内容；引导学生通过阅读厘清文本结构，掌握支撑观点的写作手法，如列举具体事例、引用专家观点和分类说明等。

二、段落解读

表1：分段解读

The original text	Interpretation
CLIMATE CHANGE REQUIRES THE WORLD'S ATTENTION	1. What do you know about climate change? The weather is becoming warmer and warmer. 2. Is climate change a good thing? No, it is said that the weather is becoming warmer and warmer.

续表

The original text	Interpretation
	3. What does "require" mean? Require means "need". It shows the situation is serious and needs attention. **4. Why should the world pay attention to climate change?** Climate change has led to problems around the world, which may become more severe and increase in number.
We have known about climate change for decades. There is little doubt that Earth is getting warmer and warmer (see the graph). A warming ocean and atmosphere along with melting ice and rising sea levels provide evidence of a dramatic change in the global climate.	**1. What signs of dramatic climate change are mentioned in the first paragraph?** A warming ocean and atmosphere, melting ice, and rising sea levels. **2. What is the purpose of this paragraph?** To introduce the topic and present the problem. **3. What does "dramatic" mean?** Dramatic means "sudden, very great, and often surprising".
In 2013, a lot of people were shocked by a news photo of a dead polar bear that was found on Norway's Arctic island of Svalbard. According to the scientists who found its dead body, all that remained of the polar bear was "skin and bones". An expert who has studied polar bears for many years said that from the position of its dead body, the bear appeared to have starved and died. Experts claimed that low sea-ice levels caused by climate change meant the bear could not hunt seals as before, so it had to travel greater distances in order to find food. This alarming	**1. What's the topic sentence of this paragraph?** This alarming case showed how the increase in temperature had an impact on Earth's ecology. **2. What shocked people?** A news photo of a dead polar bear. **3. What happened to the polar bear?** It died of hunger. **4. What possibly caused the death of the polar bear?** It couldn't find enough food. Experts claimed that low sea-ice levels caused by climate change meant the bear could not hunt seals as before, so it had to travel greater distances in order to find food. **5. What expressions are used to make the paragraph convincing?** References to specialists, like "according to the scientists …, an expert … said …, and experts claimed that …".

The original text	Interpretation
case showed how the increase in temperature had an impact on Earth's ecology.	**6. Why is this alarming case mentioned?** To serve as a supporting example of climate change and alert people to its negative impact.
Then what is causing the increase in the global average surface temperature? Climate scientists often mention a key climate process called the "greenhouse effect", which has two common meanings: the "natural" greenhouse effect and the "man-made" greenhouse effect. The "natural" greenhouse effect refers to the fact that heat from the sun enters the atmosphere and warms Earth's surface as short-wave radiation. The heat is released back into space at longer wave lengths. Greenhouse gases in the atmosphere, such as methane and carbon dioxide, trap some of the heat, keeping Earth's climate warm and habitable. Without this process, Earth could not sustain life. However, the "man-made" greenhouse effect has now become a big problem. When people produce huge amounts of extra greenhouse gases by burning fossil fuels, more heat energy is trapped in the atmosphere and causes Earth's surface temperature to rise quickly.	**1. What's the main idea of this paragraph?** It introduces the cause of global warming: the greenhouse effect. **2. How does this paragraph develop?** It develops by asking a question and answering it. **3. What types of greenhouse effect are mentioned?** There are two common types: natural and man-made. **4. What human activities produce greenhouse gases and increase the "man-made" greenhouse effect?** Burning fossil fuels like coal, oil, and natural gas. **5. Why do people burn fossil fuels?** To provide heat, generate electricity, make fuel, produce goods from raw materials, etc.

续表

The original text	Interpretation
There is strong and comprehensive evidence that the rise in temperature has led to an increase in extreme weather and natural disasters worldwide, not only causing serious damage, but also costing human lives. Climate scientists have warned that if we do not take appropriate actions, this warming trend will probably continue and there will be a higher price to pay. In fact, news reports are frequently broadcast about extreme rainstorms and heatwaves causing deaths and economic losses.	**1. What does "comprehensive" mean?** It means "including or dealing with all or nearly all elements or aspects of something". Here "comprehensive evidence" refers to many kinds of evidence. **2. What are the problems caused by global warming?** The increase in extreme weather and natural disasters worldwide not only causes serious damage but also costs human lives. **3. What's the main idea of this paragraph?** The rising temperature has resulted in serious damage.
Continued greenhouse gas emissions will result in further warming and long-lasting changes to the global climate. This requires the attention of people all over the world. Governments need to consider making policies and taking appropriate actions and measures to reduce greenhouse gas emissions. We as individuals can also reduce our "carbon footprint" by restricting the amount of carbon dioxide our lifestyles produce. It is our responsibility to seize every opportunity to educate everyone about global warming, along with its causes and impacts, because this is the most serious issue affecting all of us on this planet. So what will you do to help?	**1. What measures should be taken to deal with global warming?** (1) Governments: make policies and take appropriate actions and measures. (2) Individuals: change our lifestyles. **2. What's the purpose of this paragraph?** It is used to appeal to people all over the world. It even ends with a direct question to the reader.

表2：跨段解读

Putting it all together
1. How many parts can the text be divided into? The text can be divided into four parts. The first part includes Paragraph 1 and Paragraph 2, which talk about the problems caused by climate change. The second part includes Paragraph 3, which talks about what is causing the increase in temperature. The third part is Paragraph 4, which gives supporting evidence and further predictions. The last paragraph is the fourth part, calling for attention and action from governments and individuals. **2. Why is a polar bear mentioned?** It is used to support the writer's argument and attract people's attention. Polar bears are very popular, and this case shows the serious problems caused by climate change. **3. How does the writer connect each part?** The writer uses transitional sentences to connect each part. **4. What's the writer's tone?** It is objective, because the writer quotes a lot of news, evidence, and experts' studies. The writer doesn't use phrases like "in my opinion", "I believe", and so on. **5. How does the writer support the main idea?** The writer lists examples, quotes experts' studies, includes news reports, and makes comparisons to support the main idea of the text.

三、综合解读

综合上述分析，我们对文本进行教学设计时，应着重考量以下三个方面。

1. 语言学习

本单元阅读文本的语言学习可以围绕 "The reasons for climate change, the problems of climate change, and the solutions for climate change" 展开。教师可以引导学生按照不同表意类别梳理文本中与话题相关的词汇。具体内容如下表：

类别	词汇
通用类	greenhouse effect, global average surface temperature, atmosphere, short-wave radiation, methane, carbon dioxide, heat, ecology, etc.
原因类	burn fossil fuels, trap, rise, process, release, etc.
问题类	impact, dramatic change, extreme weather, natural disaster, economic loss, heatwave, starve, rising sea level, etc.
方案类	policy, measure, restrict, seize, etc.

此外，教师还可引导学生关注文本中相对客观的语言表达，如：There is little doubt that ...、

According to the scientists、Experts claimed that ...、There is strong and comprehensive evidence that ...、Climate scientists have warned that ... 等。学生通过复述、实践运用等活动学习这些语言表达。

2. 思维培养

在思维培养方面，教师教学可围绕 "Presenting a problem (a dramatic change in the global climate) → Giving an example (an alarming case showed how global warming had an impact on Earth's ecology) → Analysing the cause (huge amounts of extra greenhouse gases cause Earth's temperature to rise quickly) → Warning about the impact (increase in extreme weather and natural disasters causes deaths and economic losses) → Finding a solution (reduce greenhouse gas emissions, reduce our 'carbon footprint')" 这条主线展开，从问题探究入手，引导学生寻找原因，探寻解决问题的方案，熟悉"问题—原因—解决方案"类文本结构。此外，教师可引导学生思考：作为个人，我们如何帮助解决气候变暖问题？

3. 文化意识

教师应引导学生通过阅读了解气候变暖给全球人们的生活和生产带来的负面影响，认识人类活动对全球气候变化产生的巨大影响，讨论保护生态环境的重要意义，探讨不同国家在环境保护方面的做法和成功经验，思考个人在环境保护中的作用。此外，教师还要引导学生理解环境问题需要全球共同面对，培养学生的人类命运共同体意识，提升学生的责任感和担当意识。

第二节　通用版教学案例

教学内容安排：第一课时在引导学生感知全文概貌的基础上，重点处理文本第一至第三段，帮助学生了解有关全球气候变暖、温室效应的事实性信息，探究气候变暖的原因；第二课时重点处理文本第四和第五段，引导学生梳理气候变暖的后果及应对措施，提升学生的环境保护意识。

第一课时

一、课时目标

1. 通过浏览文本图表、图片和标题，预测文本内容。
2. 通过快速阅读，抓取段落关键词，获取文本基本信息，厘清文本主线，划分文本结构，明确作者的写作意图。
3. 通过细读，获取和梳理第一至第三段有关全球气候变暖、温室效应的事实性信息，并在情境中运用这些信息，表达自己的观点。

二、设计思路

本节课教师首先引导学生浏览文本中的图表，抓住"全球气温""上升"这两个信息，并通过浏览文本图片和标题，预测文本主要内容；接着引导学生通读全文，寻找段落关键词，定位相关信息，提取文本大意，梳理文本脉络，印证预测信息；之后让学生细读第一至第三段，获取主要信息和观点，理解与全球气候变暖话题相关的语言表达，学会通过读图把复杂概念简单化；然后引导学生通过采访活动，谈论相关话题，检测自己对本节课内容的掌握和运用情况；最后通过课后作业引导学生探究人们使用化石燃料的原因，把所学知识与日常生活结合起来，为第二课时探寻节能减排的方法做铺垫。

三、教学过程

Activity 1: Arousing interest in weather and climate change

本活动为实现课时目标1做铺垫。

Examine the graph on page 26 of the Student Book.

Q: What kind of information can you find in the graph?

【设计意图】引导学生观察文本中的折线图，关注升温趋势、记录年份和最大温差等关键信息。这个活动一方面激活学生已有的背景知识及相关词汇，激发学生进一步探究的兴趣；另一方面提升学生通过读图获取主要信息的能力。

【核心素养提升点】提升学生的读图能力；提升学生客观分析信息之间的关联和差异的能

力；培养学生的逻辑思维能力。

Activity 2: Predicting the content of the text

本活动旨在落实课时目标1。

1. Look at the photo in the Student Book and guess the cause of the polar bear's death.

Q1: What can you see in the photo?

Q2: What possibly caused the death of the polar bear?

2. Read the title and predict what is written in the text.

【设计意图】引导学生根据图片和标题预测文本内容。

【核心素养提升点】提升学生推断作者意图的能力；培养学生从图片和标题中获取信息的能力。

Activity 3: Reading for the main information of the text

本活动旨在落实课时目标2。

1. Skim the text and match each paragraph with a main idea.

___ Paragraph 1   A. The **impact** of global warming

___ Paragraph 2   B. The **signs** of climate change

___ Paragraph 3   C. **Solutions** to global warming

___ Paragraph 4   D. The **cause** of global warming

___ Paragraph 5   E. An alarming **case**

(BEDAC)

2. Draw the structure of the text according to the main idea of each paragraph.

Q: How many parts can the text be divided into? Why?

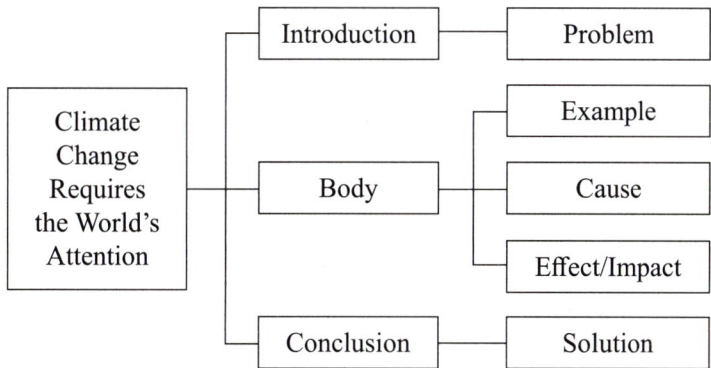

3. Determine the purpose of the text.

Q: What's the purpose of the text?

【设计意图】引导学生通过查找关键词，确定每段的段落大意；引导学生根据段落主旨划分文本结构，把握文本主线，明确作者写作意图。

【核心素养提升点】提升学生提炼主题意义的能力；提升学生对文本组织结构和文体特征的分析能力。

Activity 4: Reading for the detailed information in Paragraphs 1 to 3

本活动旨在落实课时目标3。

1. Read Paragraph 1 and find evidence.

Q: What evidence is there of dramatic climate change in the first paragraph?

(A warming ocean and atmosphere, melting ice, and rising sea levels.)

2. Read Paragraph 2 and fill in the table.

An alarming case	
When	2013
Where	Norway's Arctic island of Svalbard
Who	a polar bear
What	starved and died
Why	1. direct cause: hunger / a lack of food / food shortage 2. indirect cause: climate change

Q: What expressions are used to make the case convincing?

(References to specialists, like "According to the scientists..., An expert... said..., Experts claimed that...".)

3. Read Paragraph 3 and fill in the table.

A key climate process		
Type	"natural" greenhouse effect	"man-made" greenhouse effect
Function	keeping Earth's climate warm and habitable, and sustaining life	causing Earth's surface temperature to rise quickly
Similarity	Greenhouse gases in the atmosphere, such as methane and carbon dioxide, trap some of the heat from the sun.	
Difference	important and necessary	Huge amounts of extra greenhouse gases produced by burning fossil fuels trap more heat energy and cause Earth's surface temperature to rise quickly.

4. Look at the diagram to understand how the greenhouse effect works.

5. Think about what human activities can worsen the greenhouse effect.

Q: What human activities produce greenhouse gases and increase the "man-made" greenhouse effect?

(Burning fossil fuels like coal, oil, and natural gas.)

【设计意图】引导学生运用不同的阅读策略分析文本。例如，在分析第二段时，引导学生关注不同信息点之间的关联，使它们形成信息链；在分析第三段时，引导学生注意对比修辞手法的运用。

【核心素养提升点】培养学生厘清信息之间逻辑关系的能力；帮助学生了解作者为恰当表意所采用的引资料、作比较等写作手法。

Activity 5: Thinking and discussing

本活动旨在落实课时目标3。

Work in groups of four and design an interview.

Interviewer	a reporter from an international school newspaper
Interviewee(s)	student(s) at the international school
Topic	global warming / greenhouse effect / greenhouse gases / fossil fuels
Language	Try to use newly learnt words and expressions.
Time	7 minutes to prepare

【设计意图】引导学生把从文本中获得的信息与个人生活经历结合起来，在两者之间建立有意义的联系。

【核心素养提升点】培养学生的合作能力；提升学生的参与意识。

Assignment

1. Surf the Internet and find 3 or 4 reasons why people burn fossil fuels.
2. Read Paragraph 3 again and create your own diagram that shows how the greenhouse effect works.
3. Finish part of the worksheet.

【设计意图】引导学生通过网络检索查找语言学习所需的材料，丰富对人为温室效应的认知，并为第二课时的迁移创新类活动搭好脚手架；引导学生用示意图将复杂信息可视化，学会借助图表等非语言信息进行表达。

【核心素养提升点】提升学生主动学习的能力；培养学生运用图表进行表达的能力。

附: Worksheet

Unit 3 Reading and Thinking

1. Read for the structure.

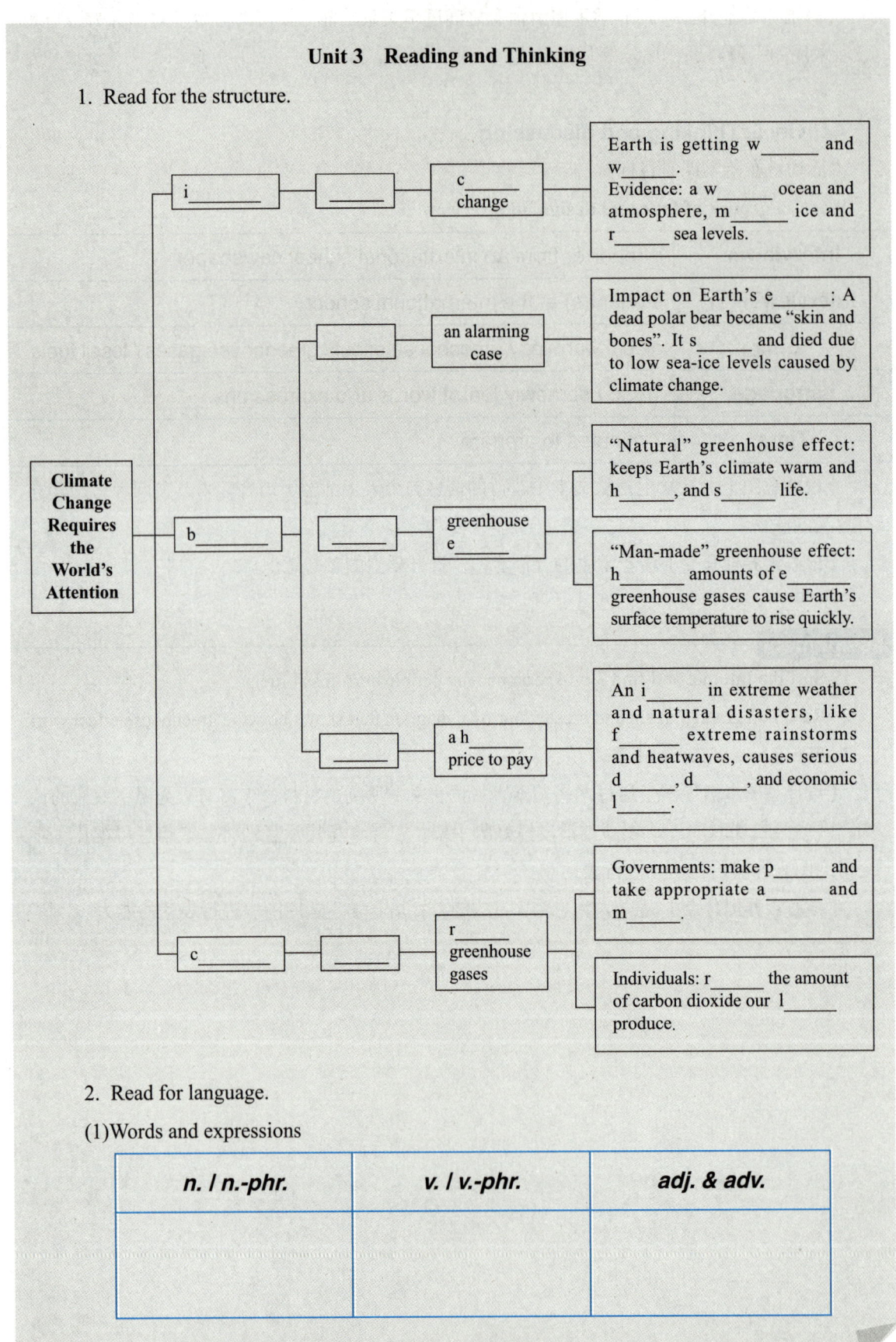

Climate Change Requires the World's Attention
- i_____ → _____ → c_____ change → Earth is getting w_____ and w_____. Evidence: a w_____ ocean and atmosphere, m_____ ice and r_____ sea levels.
- b_____
  - _____ → an alarming case → Impact on Earth's e_____: A dead polar bear became "skin and bones". It s_____ and died due to low sea-ice levels caused by climate change.
  - _____ → greenhouse e_____ →
    - "Natural" greenhouse effect: keeps Earth's climate warm and h_____, and s_____ life.
    - "Man-made" greenhouse effect: h_____ amounts of e_____ greenhouse gases cause Earth's surface temperature to rise quickly.
  - _____ → a h_____ price to pay → An i_____ in extreme weather and natural disasters, like f_____ extreme rainstorms and heatwaves, causes serious d_____, d_____, and economic l_____.
- c_____ → _____ → r_____ greenhouse gases →
  - Governments: make p_____ and take appropriate a_____ and m_____.
  - Individuals: r_____ the amount of carbon dioxide our l_____ produce.

2. Read for language.

(1) Words and expressions

n. / n.-phr.	v. / v.-phr.	adj. & adv.

58 | UNIT 3 ENVIRONMENTAL PROTECTION |

(2) Sentence pattern

There _____

There _____

3. Read for the meaning.

Q1: What is the purpose of writing this text?
_____

Q2: Why do people use fossil fuels?
_____

四、教学反思

本节课目标主要包括浏览图表、图片和标题，预测文本内容；抓取段落关键词，提取文本大意，划分文本结构；梳理第一至第三段，获取相关信息并加以运用。从教学效果看，在读图环节，由于图表和图片直观性强，学生普遍比较感兴趣，能够积极思考和表达。在段落大意连线环节，学生完成得比较轻松，但是在划分文本结构及归纳作者写作意图时，学生完成起来有一定难度。在细读文本第一至第三段时，教师引导学生通过回答问题、填表、对比、看图等多种形式进行文本分析，帮助学生梳理整合相关信息。

本节课还有一些不足之处。其一，在确定段落大意环节，学生其实能够通过阅读技巧从段首或段尾找出段落关键词，因此教师不必为了降低难度而将此环节设置成连线题，这样反而没有锻炼学生的概括能力。其二，在采访环节，三组学生的课堂表现体现出了一个共性问题，即对本节课新学词汇和句型的使用不够充分。这可能与活动前教师给的指令语"Try to use newly learnt words and expressions."不够明确有关。因此，教师应该给出具体要求，比如学生应至少使用三个新学词汇或句型；或者，在小组准备时，教师走动指导，及时指出不足、提出改进建议。

第二课时

一、课时目标

1. 展示优秀作业，复述第一课时的重点内容。

2. 通过细读，梳理全球气候变暖的后果、应对措施以及作者对全球气候变暖的态度等相关信息。

3. 通过个人思考、小组合作、同伴分享，用给作者写信的方式分享日常生活中切实可行的减少碳排放的方法。

二、设计思路

本节课教学重点落实"实践与内化、迁移与创新"。教师首先让学生交流课后作业,回顾第一课时的重点内容,尤其是对温室效应的理解,并分享自己课后搜集到的人们使用化石燃料的原因;然后引导学生细读文本第四和第五段,通过表格形式,分类梳理全球气候变暖的后果和应对措施等相关信息;最后引导学生通过给作者写信,分享日常生活中切实可行的减少碳排放的方法。

三、教学过程

Activity 1: Reviewing the assignment

本活动旨在落实课时目标1。

1. Share your diagram that shows how the greenhouse effect works.

T: Each group picks out the best diagram in its group. One member sticks it on the blackboard and gives a short explanation of how the greenhouse effect works.

2. Show the answers to the question "Why do people burn fossil fuels?" and then categorise them.

> 【设计意图】步骤1让学生通过展示自己小组的最佳示意图,进一步练习用英语阐述温室效应的原理,深度理解全球气候变暖的原因。步骤2让学生分享自己搜集到的人们使用化石燃料的原因,为后面活动3做好铺垫。
>
> 【核心素养提升点】提升学生解读和绘制示意图的能力;提升学生的语言表达能力。

Activity 2: Reading for the detailed information in Paragraphs 4 and 5

本活动旨在落实课时目标2。

1. Read Paragraph 4 and find the problems caused by global warming.

Q: What examples of extreme weather and natural disasters do you know, and what are their effects?

Extreme weather and natural disasters	
Example	Effect
extreme rainstorms extreme heatwaves floods droughts earthquakes …	deaths economic losses …

2. **Read Paragraph 5 and find the measures that should be taken to deal with global warming.**

Q: What measures should be taken to deal with global warming?

Measure	
Government **To reduce greenhouse gas emissions**	**Individual** **To reduce "carbon footprint"**
Make policies. Take appropriate actions and measures.	Change inappropriate lifestyles. Seize every opportunity to educate everyone.

【设计意图】通过问题和表格，帮助学生梳理文本信息。

【核心素养提升点】提升学生分析信息之间关联的能力；提升学生归纳信息的能力。

Activity 3: Thinking and writing

本活动旨在落实课时目标3。

1. **Write a letter to the writer about what you will do to help.**

   - Pick one topic from the previous presentation in Activity 1.
   - Use "1+2+3 method" (1 sentence pattern, 2 phrases, 3 *n./v./adj.* learnt from the text).
   - Write 60–80 words within 10 minutes.

2. **Appreciate the quote on the Opening Page.**

【设计意图】步骤1引导学生通过合作探究，在新的语境中运用所学语言，给作者写信分享自己为减少碳排放将采取的措施。这个活动帮助学生与文本、与作者形成互动。步骤2引导学生关注单元开篇页的名言，理解人类要和自然和谐共生，并把所学所悟迁移到自己的日常生活中，提升环境保护意识，增强社会责任感。

【核心素养提升点】帮助学生学会分析、判断他人观点和思想，并形成自己的观点；帮助学生树立正确的价值观。

Assignment

1. Polish your letter to the writer.
2. Complete the worksheet.

【设计意图】引导学生在新的语境中运用所学语言，提升环境保护意识。

【核心素养提升点】提升学生陈述事件、传递信息的能力；培养学生表达个人观点和情感的能力。

附: **Worksheet**

Unit 3   Reading and Thinking

1. Summarise the text's words and expressions.

n. / n.-phr.	v. / v.-phr.	adj. & adv.	Sentence pattern

2. Summarise the writer's suggestions.

Government	Individual

3. Write a letter.

Dear writer,

    There is strong evidence that burning fossil fuels produces extra greenhouse gases and worsens global warming. We should take immediate actions to reduce greenhouse gas emissions.

    First, I will restrict my use of energy by turning off the light when leaving a room. Second, I will tell my parents to buy a solar water heater to replace the gas water heater. Third, in winter, I will try to use the electric heater less and wear more clothes instead.

    All in all, I will seize every opportunity to reduce my "carbon footprint". Thank you for educating us about global warming.

Yours,
Reader

Dear writer,

_____
_____
_____
_____

Yours,
Reader

四、教学反思

本节课教学目标达成情况较好。在第一个环节，作业展示有效地吸引了学生的注意力，帮助学生回顾了第一课时的学习内容。在第二个环节，教师引导学生以表格的形式，分类梳理第四和第五段主要信息。学生都能够准确找到关键信息。在最后的写作环节，教师提供了参考范文，降低了学生的写作难度。

本节课的不足主要体现在写作环节。学生虽然能在规定时间内完成写作任务，但写作质量并不高。写作任务要求学生从第一课时的作业，即从所搜集到的人们使用化石燃料的原因中，找到一个切入点，分享一些能够减少碳排放的方法。但是，学生往往从多个原因切入，所写的内容较为分散，叙述不够详细。教师应引导学生在阅读范文后，对照写作要求，着重分析范文是如何围绕一个点展开叙述的。教师还可以用思维导图列出写作要点和它们之间的逻辑关系，引导学生构思写作。

第三节　提高版教学案例

教学内容安排：第一课时引导学生理解全文，梳理文本结构，重点关注全球气候变暖的原因和后果；第二课时引导学生聚焦文本续写，整理课前搜集的素材，依据文本特点进行仿写。

第一课时

一、课时目标

1. 了解文本主要内容，梳理文本结构。
2. 通过阅读文本和绘制图表，探究全球气候变暖的原因和后果。
3. 通过进一步阅读和思考，探索减缓全球气候变暖进程的有效方法。

二、设计思路

本节课采用整体阅读教学，先全局再局部，围绕"提出问题—激发兴趣—厘清结构—获取信息—内化信息—输出表达—思考问题解决方案"展开。教师首先从文本中的图片入手，通过提问"为什么北极熊死了？"引导学生聚焦主题，激发学生的阅读兴趣；接着引导学生通过略读，厘清文本结构，从整体上把握文本信息；然后让学生通过详细阅读，获取目标信息，了解全球气候变暖的原因和后果，并通过绘制示意图和思维导图，形象地呈现文本信息，实现语言的内化；最后引导学生思考如何应对全球气候变暖问题，为第二课时的学习打好基础。

三、教学过程

Activity 1: Discussing the graph and photo

本活动为实现课时目标1做铺垫。

1. Describe the graph and news photo, and then predict the content of the text.

Q1: What can you say about the graph and the news photo?

Q2: What happened to the polar bear in the photo?

Q3: What's the possible relationship between the temperature and the bear?

Q4: Can you predict what may be talked about in the text?

【设计意图】引导学生通过描述图表和图片内容，思考气候发生的变化，以及北极熊死亡的原因，激发学生继续探究的兴趣，培养他们"看"图说话的能力；引导学生预测文本内容，为后续的阅读活动做铺垫。

【核心素养提升点】培养学生的读图能力；培养学生独立思考的能力。

2. Read the first two paragraphs and find what is said about the graph and the photo to check your prediction.

Q1: What does the writer say about the graph?

Q2: What does the writer say about the polar bear?

Q3: What kind of case is it?

Q4: According to the text, what does the alarming case show?

3. Think about the effect of and reasons for climate change.

Q1: What types of extreme weather and natural disasters do you know?

Q2: Do you think climate change is the result of human activity? Give your reasons.

> 【设计意图】引导学生围绕预测展开阅读，验证预测并思考与文本主题相关的问题，进一步探索主题语境的意义。
>
> 【核心素养提升点】提升学生的语言表达能力；提升学生的预测能力；培养学生深度思考的能力。

Activity 2: Clarifying the structure

本活动旨在落实课时目标1。

Skim the text and label the paragraphs with the correct key words to clarify the structure of the text.

Paragraph	Key word
1	
2	
3	
4	
5	

(Key words: problem, example, reason, evidence, solution.)

> 【设计意图】引导学生通过略读确定每段的关键词，了解每段表达的主题，同时验证预测信息。
>
> 【核心素养提升点】培养学生快速查找关键信息的能力；提升学生分析文本结构的能力。

Activity 3: Digging for reasons

本活动旨在落实课时目标2。

1. Find the reasons for climate change.

Q1: What is causing the increase in the global average surface temperature?

Q2: What are the two common meanings of greenhouse effect?

Q3: What does the "natural" greenhouse effect refer to?

2. Work in groups to create a diagram that shows how the greenhouse effect works.

3. Present the diagram.

【设计意图】引导学生带着目标进行阅读，查找信息并通过回答问题明确信息，并将这些信息与自己在活动1中对于全球气候变暖原因的思考进行比较，验证自己先前的回答，拓展思路；引导学生通过绘制示意图，学习表达信息的新方式，内化所学内容。

【核心素养提升点】提升学生获取信息的能力；培养学生绘制示意图的能力。

Activity 4: Understanding the problem

本活动旨在落实课时目标2。

1. Talk about the "man-made" greenhouse effect.

Q1: What does the "man-made" greenhouse effect refer to?

Q2: What do you think about the "man-made" greenhouse effect?

2. Read the text again and find the problems caused by climate change.

Q: What are the problems caused by climate change?

3. Draw a mind map to present your findings.

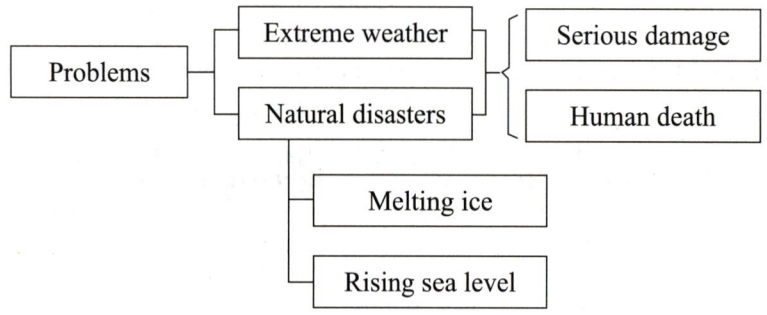

【设计意图】引导学生带着目标再读文本，获取相关信息，并通过绘制思维导图，对信息进行梳理和表达，同时将这些信息与自己在活动1中对于全球气候变暖后果的思考进行比较，验证自己先前的回答，拓展思路。

【核心素养提升点】提升学生获取与运用信息的能力；培养学生绘制思维导图的能力。

Activity 5: Seeking solutions

本活动旨在落实课时目标3。

Find the solutions suggested in the last paragraph, and think about more solutions to the problem.

Q1: What solutions are suggested in the last paragraph?

Q2: What more could you do to help?

【设计意图】引导学生探究问题解决方案，再次进行深入思考，为课后作业和第二课时的学习做好准备。

【核心素养提升点】提升学生的思考能力；提升学生解决问题的能力。

> **Assignment**
>
> 1. Do a survey to find out what people's opinions on climate change are and what they can do to help.
> 2. Surf online to find more ways in which we can help.
>
> 【设计意图】让学生通过调查和网络检索获取信息，为第二课时的写作活动做好准备。
>
> 【核心素养提升点】提升学生的交际能力；培养学生的思辨能力；提升学生的信息搜索能力。

四、教学反思

本节课学生在主题语境的引领下，通过学习理解和应用实践活动，梳理全球气候变暖的原因及后果，整体教学目标达成度较高。首先，本节课锻炼了学生的语言表达能力。从"看"图说话，到迁移运用示意图，再到描述气候变暖带来的问题，每一个环节都在促使学生不断地使用语言进行表达，通过"说"表达自己的理解，内化所学。其次，本节课注重培养学生的学习能力。一些教学活动，如对图片和图表的分析和解读、从整体到局部的文本解读，以及图表绘制等，让学生体会不同的学习方法，引导学生在文本信息预测、解读以及梳理等方面养成良好的学习习惯，帮助学生提升学习能力。

本节课还应进一步加强对学生思考能力的培养。相对而言，环境问题与学生的实际生活相距较远，且涉及较多专业知识。因此，除文本中的图表和图片外，教师还应补充一些相关的音像资料，以充实语境，启发学生思考。

第二课时

一、课时目标

1. 整理和分享所搜集的素材，激活思维，为续写搭建内容支架。
2. 进一步分析文本语言特点和篇章结构，为续写搭建语言支架。
3. 通过写作，内化所学并迁移创新，提升文本赏析能力和语言表达能力。

二、设计思路

本节课重点围绕续写活动展开。教师引导学生深入分析文本，掌握文本的语言特点和篇章结构，并结合课前搜集的素材完成续写任务。教师首先让学生分享第一课时的课后作业，回顾文本最后提到的问题，思考如何完成续写；接着引导学生分析文本语言特点，把握语言风格，特别注意关注段落间的过渡句，为续写做好语言方面的准备；然后引导学生在明确写作技巧的基础上，开展写作活动，完成续写任务；最后引导学生通过同伴互评，进一步内化所学，提升文本赏析能力，培养环保意识。课后作业要求学生上网搜索中国在应对环境问题上所采取的措施和所做的贡献，帮助学生学会用英语讲述中国故事，进一步提升学生的文化意识，培养学生的家国情怀。

三、教学过程

Activity 1: Checking the assignment

本活动旨在落实课时目标1。

1. Review the assignment and share what you have found in pairs.

2. Think about how you could continue the text.

Q: What would you write if you were to continue the text?

【设计意图】引导学生回顾第一课时所学，检验自己作业完成的情况，为续写搭建内容支架，同时明晰本节课写作任务。

【核心素养提升点】提升学生的语言表达能力。

Activity 2: Focusing on the tone

本活动旨在落实课时目标2。

1. In pairs, discuss the tone of the text.

Q: Is the tone of the text subjective or objective? Why?

2. Find out how the writer presents the information.

Phrase	Information
E.g. There is little doubt that ...	melting ice and rising sea level
	a dead polar bear found
	how the polar bear died
	two common meanings of the greenhouse effect
	extreme weather and natural disasters worldwide
	warming trend will probably continue
	extreme rainstorms and heatwaves

3. Make a choice between two descriptions to check your understanding of the tone.

【设计意图】引导学生细读文本，思考和探究文本的语言风格，为续写做好语言上的准备。

【核心素养提升点】培养学生的思辨能力；提升学生的语言分析能力。

Activity 3: Discussing the language pattern

本活动旨在落实课时目标2。

1. Analyse the language pattern in the text.

Q1: Please take a closer look at the language—what features can you find?

Q2: Is there indirect speech?

2. Find examples of indirect speech in the text.

【设计意图】引导学生思考和探究文本的语言特点，掌握间接引语的表达方式。

【核心素养提升点】培养学生的思辨能力；提升学生的语言分析能力。

Activity 4: Understanding the transition between paragraphs

本活动旨在落实课时目标2。

1. Examine the transitional words or sentences between the paragraphs.

2. Discuss what could be talked about next in the text, and write down a transitional sentence to connect the last paragraph.

T: For the next paragraph, you could write some suggestions, and your transitional sentence could be "Here are some tips suggested by experts that we individuals can use to help to deal with the most serious issue."

【设计意图】引导学生关注文本段落之间的衔接，开展关于过渡句的微写作训练，同时思考如何让续写文本自然接续前面的内容。

【核心素养提升点】帮助学生感知文本段落之间的衔接方式；提升学生的语言分析能力。

Activity 5: Continuation writing

本活动旨在落实课时目标3。

1. Write a paragraph of about 80 words using the material collected and tips learnt.

2. Assess your paragraph in pairs using the assessment sheet.

Assessment sheet		
Item	Good	Need improving
1. Comparatively objective tone		
2. Indirect speech		
3. Transitional sentence or words		

3. Explain your assessment to your partner.

【设计意图】引导学生通过续写，内化所学的写作技巧，顺利实现对语言的迁移运用；引导学生通过评价同伴作文，提升文本赏析能力，并进一步内化所学，提升环保意识。

【核心素养提升点】提升学生的语言表达能力；提升学生的文本赏析能力。

Assignment

1. Improve your writing based on the comments you received.

2. Search online for information about "China is going green", and take notes on and appreciate how China is dealing with climate change.

【设计意图】让学生继续完善作文，并了解中国在应对环境问题上所采取的措施和所做的贡献。

【核心素养提升点】提升学生的语言表达能力；帮助学生学会用英语讲述中国故事；提升学生的文化意识；培养学生的家国情怀。

The teacher's version:

Here are some experts' suggestions to address the issue. To start with, consider greener ways of getting around. It is reported that transportation accounts for about 24 percent of carbon dioxide emissions, so changing the way you travel matters a lot. Besides this, use energy wisely. It may seem obvious, but many people overlook it, and experts say it could make a huge difference if everybody becomes energy aware. We all need to begin taking action now, or there'll be more and more sad cases like the polar bear.

四、教学反思

本节课聚焦文本续写，通过续写训练学生深度解读文本的能力以及思辨能力，帮助学生提升环保意识，塑造文化品格。本节课有两大亮点。第一，支架搭建合理。续写是对文本的延续写作，需要学生深入理解阅读文本的语言特点。该文本通过间接引语的方式引用了科学家、环保专家的观点以及新闻报道的信息，表述较为客观。学生对这些语言信息进行分析，为续写活动搭建了语言支架。第二，任务真实有趣。续写的内容来自学生自己的课后调查。这样的安排激发了学生的兴趣，调动了学生的积极性。同时，这一任务也让学生看到英语学习在现实生活中发挥的作用，从而进一步激发学生学习英语的动力。

限时写作一直是学生倍感压力的环节，因此合理搭建写作支架、缓解写作压力非常重要。建议在第一个环节，教师不仅要给学生充分的时间进行素材分享，还要引导学生对素材进行详细梳理。此外，对于最后环节中的同伴评价，如果学生理解不到位，评价过程容易流于形式。建议教师在同伴评价前，引导学生明白评价的重要性，同时在评价的过程中给予充分的指导，提示学生围绕要点展开评价，这样可以有效地提高评价质量。

UNIT 4　ADVERSITY AND COURAGE
Reading and Thinking　A SUCCESSFUL FAILURE

第一节　文本解读

一、总体解读

本单元的主题是"逆境与勇气"。阅读文本"A Successful Failure"的主体部分是三则日记，以叙事为主，讲述英国探险家沙克尔顿带领一支28人的探险队乘坐"坚忍号"远征南极，被困长达两年，历经磨难却不放弃，最终全部生还的经过。该文本旨在让高中学生了解20世纪一次伟大的南极探险经历，以及船长沙克尔顿在极度恶劣的环境下冷静应对的处事方式、坚韧不拔的精神和高超的领导能力，帮助学生学会以勇于探索、顽强拼搏的心态去迎接生活中的种种考验。

该文本分为两个部分，一部分是背景知识介绍，另一部分是以"坚忍号"服务员珀西·布莱克博罗的口吻写下的三则日记。三则日记的前后时间跨度很大，但从内容上看，它们记录了探险历程中的几次重大事件，勾勒了这次南极探险的基本故事脉络。第一则日记主要内容是十九岁的少年珀西因为对沙克尔顿船长的崇拜以及对海上探险的渴望，悄悄登上"坚忍号"，被沙克尔顿发现后被指派为船上的服务员，负责为船员们做饭。第二则日记主要内容是"坚忍号"被浮冰围困后，沙克尔顿冷静又有条理地组织船员应对危机。他果断带领船员们弃船自救，暂居浮冰之上。第三则日记主要内容是船员们流落到荒无人烟的象岛，在严酷的自然环境下艰难求生；沙克尔顿组织救援小队赴南乔治亚岛寻求帮助。

主要人物珀西的年龄与高中学生相近，文本又以日记的方式呈现探险队经历的磨难，这使得文本内容和立意容易为学生所接受，进而让学生产生共鸣。标题"A Successful Failure"是整个文本的浓缩提炼，说明探险队经历生死考验，虽然没有到达原本的目的地，但在沙克尔顿的正确指挥下平安归来。该文本还使用了一些心理描写和对话，生动描绘了恶劣的环境，并且展现了沙克尔顿的人格魅力以及他在队员中传递的公正、关爱他人的高尚品质和坚韧不拔的精神力量。

在阅读策略方面，教师可以引导学生借助招募广告预测文本内容；引导学生对文本中的细节信息进行推理分析，判断人物的心理状态和性格品质。

二、段落解读

表1：分段解读

The original text	Interpretation
MEN WANTED for a dangerous journey: small wages, bitter cold, long months of complete darkness, constant danger, and safe return uncertain. Honour and reward will follow if it is successful. Ernest Shackleton	**1. What information can we get from the advertisement?** It is an advert looking for men to go on a rewarding and honorable journey, which would be dangerous, cold, dark, long, and full of uncertainty. **2. Who was wanting men? What kind of men were wanted?** Ernest Shackleton was recruiting men / crew members, and they needed to be brave, adventurous, and experienced. **3. What can be inferred about Ernest Shackleton?** He was an honest, adventurous, thoughtful, and experienced captain.
A SUCCESSFUL FAILURE	**1. Which two words have opposite meanings?** "Successful" and "Failure". **2. What figure of speech is it?** Oxymoron. **3. Whose failure was it and who succeeded?** Maybe it was the failure of Shackleton and his team, but they were successful because they didn't die.
Perce Blackborow joined an expedition with Sir Ernest Shackleton to Antarctica on the ship *Endurance* in 1914. Shackleton was one of the most famous explorers of his day and it was considered a great honour to be part of his expeditions. Below are some of Blackborow's diary entries.	**1. Who were on board the ship *Endurance*?** Perce Blackborow, Sir Ernest Shackleton, and other men. **2. What did they do?** They went on an expedition. **3. Where and when did they go?** To Antarctica, in 1914. **4. For what purpose did they go there?** Perhaps to explore the unknown. **5. Why was it a great honour to be part of Shackleton's expeditions?** Because he was one of the most famous explorers of his day.

续表

The original text	Interpretation
31 Oct 1914 ... Well, it so happened that one morning I bought a newspaper and read the advertisement about the Antarctic expedition. An expedition to the South Pole with the great Sir Ernest Shackleton—this is the adventure that I have been dreaming of. And I was ready for it. At the age of 19, I am fit and full of vigour. However, when I applied to join the expedition, Shackleton turned me down because he thought I was too young and wasn't qualified. But I was so enthusiastic about the idea of going along with them that I secretly went aboard his ship, the *Endurance*, and hid in a small cupboard. Unfortunately, three days after we set off I was discovered. Shackleton did not want to turn back so he offered me a job, but only after he promised me, "If anyone has to be eaten, then you will be the first!" He assigned me to be a steward, and I now serve meals for twenty-eight men, three times a day. How everyone will envy me when I come back and tell them about the amazing places I have been to!	**1. What is the date and location of the diary entry?** 31 Oct 1914, while at sea. **2. What is this diary entry about?** How "I" (Blackborow) joined the expedition. **3. What does the sentence "this is the adventure that I have been dreaming of" tell you about Blackborow?** He was enthusiastic, brave, and eager for adventure. **4. What can we learn about Blackborow from the sentence "At the age of 19, I am fit and full of vigour"?** He was young, healthy, confident, and energetic. **5. What made Blackborow secretly go aboard the ship?** First, he was turned down by Shackleton. Second, he had a strong desire for adventure and was determined to join the expedition. **6. How did Shackleton handle the situation when Blackborow got discovered?** He kept sailing and assigned Blackborow to serve as a steward. **7. What does "promised me" mean here? Why did Shackleton do so?** It means "warned me". He wanted to remain just and fair to those already on board, as they had all been strictly selected, while Blackborow was unqualified. **8. What can we infer about Blackborow's feelings from the last sentence?** He was proud and excited, and maybe a bit innocent too. **9. What phrases are used to describe young Blackborow?** The phrases are "full of vigour" and "enthusiastic about".
21 Nov 1915 The journey has not been easy. *Endurance* became stuck in the ice as we approached Antarctica. The ice froze around us and we	**1. What is the date and location of the diary entry?** 21 Nov 1915, on floating ice. **2. What is this diary entry about?** How "we" got stuck, abandoned the ship, and camped on the ice.

The original text	Interpretation
were well and truly stuck! We saw the ship get crushed by the ice. And when the ship sank, our hearts sank with it. Before we abandoned the ship, Shackleton calmly called us together and told us to rescue our most essential supplies—the small boats, our food, the cook stove, candles, clothes, and blankets. This was no time to panic. We were not allowed to take most of our personal belongings, and Shackleton himself threw away all his gold. But to our surprise, he allowed Hussey to keep his banjo. Hussey often plays it to keep our spirits up. We are now camped on the ice and we have been managing to survive, but spring is coming, and the ice will soon begin to melt.	**3. What phrases are used to describe their adversity?** Became stuck in, ice froze around us, well and truly stuck, get crushed by, our hearts sank. **4. How did they feel when the ship sank?** Their hearts sank with it, so they were depressed and sad. **5. How did Shackleton behave in the face of such adversity?** Calmly and logically. **6. What does the sentence "(he) told us to rescue our most essential supplies" infer about Shackleton?** He was calm, sensible, and experienced. **7. Why did Shackleton throw away all his gold?** He wanted to lead by example. **8. Why did Shackleton allow Hussey to keep his banjo?** He was aware that music could keep the crew's spirits up. **9. What expressions are used to describe Shackleton's orders? What kind of leadership can be inferred?** Calmly called us together, told us to rescue, were not allowed to, allowed Hussey to keep. It can be inferred that Shackleton was an experienced captain with authority. **10. What can we infer about the crew from the description "we have been managing to survive"?** "Have been doing something" is used when someone has kept doing something for a period of time. "We have been managing to survive" means they had successfully overcome the difficulties of camping on ice. The use of present perfect continuous tense and the word "manage" together shows that the crew members were persevering, united, intelligent, and strong-willed. And it also infers that the difficulty was ongoing, meaning that they had to struggle to survive each day.

The original text	Interpretation
20 May 1916 We have been struggling for days, but things on Elephant Island are going from bad to worse. We are now crowded together under one of our boats on the rocky shore of this miserable place. Soon after we arrived, Shackleton left us to find help on South Georgia Island, 1,320 kilometres away—the voyage was too dangerous and difficult for all of us to make it in our small boats. If Shackleton fails, will we have any hope of rescue? No. No navy in the world ever stops at Elephant Island, and no one else knows that we are here. I feel low. It's cold and windy. The island has no plants. Sometimes we are able to catch a seal or a penguin to eat. Otherwise, there is no food. I try to think of happier things: decent food, warm and dry clothes, a cosy bedroom, sunny days, and my mother's face … However, these happy memories are soon interrupted by a sudden cold rush of air. I shouted, "Shut the door!" "Hold on now, Perce. Don't you go turning into another Tom," came the reply. "We've caught another penguin, so it's penguin soup tonight!" Bless Frank Wild, the kindest man there is after our leader, Ernest Shackleton. How could I become as selfish and bad-tempered as Thomas Orde-Lees!	**1. What is the date and location of the diary entry?** 20 May 1916, on Elephant Island. **2. What is this diary entry about?** How "we" waited for rescue and struggled to survive. **3. What was Elephant Island like?** A cold, windy, and miserable place with rocky shores and no plants. **4. What does "We have been struggling for days" tell us about the crew members?** The crew members were finding it very difficult to survive. In the last entry, they were "managing to survive", but now "things are going from bad to worse". **5. According to the diary entry, "the voyage was too dangerous and difficult for all of us to make it in our small boats". So why did Shackleton choose to make the voyage himself?** He was determined to take the crew back home, and he knew he had to make sure the voyage would succeed. And he always led by example. **6. What made Blackborow feel low?** Being crowded under one of their boats on the miserable island, the cold, the hunger, and the uncertainty of rescue. **7. Blackborow said, "I try to think of happier things …" What kind of person was Blackborow?** He was optimistic and innocent. **8. According to the descriptions in this diary, what kind of person was Frank Wild?** Kind, caring, patient, and optimistic. **9. Besides feeling low, what other feelings do you think Blackborow had on the island?** Worried, uncertain, but hopeful.

续表

The original text	Interpretation
Without Frank and Ernest, we'd all be dead by now. Their genuine concern for others, their perseverance, and their resolve fill me with hope. Perhaps there is a chance we will return home, after all.	

表2：跨段解读

Putting it all together

1. What do the three diary entries tell us about Blackborow's experience on the *Endurance*?

They tell us about how Blackborow joined the expedition to Antarctica, the hardships he and other crew members went through, and the qualities they showed in the face of adversity.

2. How did Blackborow's feelings change over time?

He was enthusiastic, eager, and confident before going on board the ship, and he was excited and proud when the ship set sail. Later, when they were camping on the ice, he became depressed and worried. While he was waiting to be rescued from Elephant Island, he felt worried, uncertain, and low, but still hopeful.

3. What different words and phrases does the writer use to describe adversity, people, and emotions?

(1) Adversity: become stuck in, be well and truly stuck, get crushed by, this is no time to panic, things go from bad to worse, etc.

(2) People: be full of vigour, be enthusiastic about, selfish and bad-tempered, the kindest, genuine concern for others, perseverance, etc.

(3) Emotions: our hearts sink, to one's surprise, feel low, Bless …, calmly, fill sb with hope, etc.

4. What qualities shown by the characters are most needed for overcoming adversity?

Determination, perseverance, confidence, calmness, genuine care for others, courage, optimism, and leading by example, etc.

三、综合解读

综合上述分析，我们对文本进行教学设计时，应着重考量以下三个方面。

1. 语言学习

教师可以引导学生围绕"逆境"和"坚毅"两个关键词梳理相关的语言表达，如become stuck in、be well and truly stuck、get crushed by、this is no time to panic、keep one's spirits up、things go from bad to worse、have hope of rescue、be full of vigour、be enthusiastic about、have genuine concern for others、our hearts sink、to one's surprise、feel low、fill sb with hope等。在阅读教学中，教师既要帮助学生处理一些与话题相关的"生词"，也要关注部分学生眼中的"老词"，特别是那些需要通过上下文语境才能确定意义的词汇，如第一则日记中的promise。

2. 思维培养

三则日记依次描述"坚忍号"南极探险历程中的三个重大事件。多处细节信息反映了日记主人心理状态的变化，展示了相关人物的性格品质。教师要引导学生抓住重大事件和心理状态的变化这两条明暗主线，梳理文本，系统化地处理信息，培养逻辑思维能力。教师还要带领学生进一步分析探险队几个主要人物的性格品质，梳理和总结应对逆境的必备品质。教师还可以布置写作任务，如写瓶中信或描述自己经历过的一次逆境，分享自己如何战胜困难、走出困境。

3. 文化意识

文本以日记的方式呈现探险队经历的磨难，从侧面刻画了探险过程中的典型人物，内容真实，容易引起学生的共鸣。教师要引导学生了解典型人物面对逆境时表现出来的坚毅品质和乐观精神，帮助学生学会正视困难，勇于挑战自我，以坚韧不拔的毅力面对人生的逆境和挫折。

第二节　通用版教学案例

教学内容安排：第一课时引导学生整体阅读文本，理解文本关键信息；第二课时引导学生赏析优秀习作，深入理解文本，推断和总结探险队主要人物的优秀品质，最后通过角色扮演活动实现对所学语言的迁移与运用。

第一课时

一、课时目标

1. 通过浏览和讨论图片内容以及招募广告信息，激活背景知识和相关话题语言，预测文本内容。
2. 通过寻读和略读文本，梳理归纳文本主要内容，理解关键信息，概括三则日记的大意。
3. 通过分析描述情绪变化的语言表达，推断人物心理状态的变化，培养逻辑思维能力。

二、设计思路

本节课的重点是理解文本信息。教师首先通过问题"When to go / How to go / What to do if you plan to travel to Antarctica？"和"If you set off from London for the expedition, what route would you take？"，引导学生结合图片讨论南极旅游相关内容，导入本节课话题，激发学生的阅读兴趣；接着让学生阅读招募广告，预测文本内容；之后通过设置5W1H的表格任务，引导学生寻读文本，获取基本信息；然后让学生略读三则日记，梳理和归纳每则日记的写作日期、写作地点和大意；最后引导学生分析和提炼主人公珀西在探险历程中心理状态的变化。本节课的课后作业为完成概括文本大意的填空训练，以及以珀西的口吻写一封瓶中信，为第二课时的写作微技能训练做好铺垫。

三、教学过程

Activity 1: Talking about travelling to Antarctica

本活动旨在落实课时目标1。

1. Revise the names of continents and learn the new word "Antarctica".

Q1: How many continents are there? What are they?

Q2: What's the Earth's southernmost continent called?

2. In pairs, talk about travelling to Antarctica.

Q1: When is the best time for us to go there?

Q2: How can we go there?

Q3: What can we do there?

Q4: If you set off from London for an expedition to Antarctica, what route would you take?

【设计意图】引导学生认识南极洲的名称，然后结合图片就第二个任务的四个问题进行讨论，激活背景知识，引出penguin、bitter cold、long months of darkness、by ship等话题词汇，为后续阅读活动做好准备。

【核心素养提升点】提升学生的语言表达能力。

Activity 2: Inquiring about the advertisement to predict the content of the text

本活动旨在落实课时目标1。

Look through the advertisement and answer the following questions.

Q1: What information can you get?

Q2: Will you apply if you are seeking a job? Why?

Q3: What extra information would you want to know about the expedition?

【设计意图】引导学生浏览和讨论招募广告的内容，梳理从中获取的信息，预测文本内容，聚焦主题语境。

【核心素养提升点】培养学生的推断能力；提升学生主动学习的能力。

Activity 3: Identifying the key information of the expedition

本活动旨在落实课时目标2。

1. Scan Paragraph 1 to find out the key information of the text.

Who	Perce Blackborow, Sir Ernest Shackleton, other crew members
What	an expedition
Where	Antarctica
When	from 1914 to 1916
How	by sea (on the ship *Endurance*)
Why	to explore the unknown

2. Skim the three diary entries and write the location and main idea of each one by using "I" or "we" with a limit of 8 words.

Diary date	Location	Main idea
31 Oct 1914	at sea	"I" joined the expedition.
21 Nov 1915	on floating ice	"We" got stuck and abandoned the ship.
20 May 1916	on Elephant Island	Waiting for rescue, "we" struggled to survive.

【设计意图】步骤1引导学生运用寻读策略，整体梳理文本内容。步骤2让学生略读三则日记，概括日记大意，提炼和重构信息。

【核心素养提升点】培养学生整体把握文本内容的能力；提升学生提炼和重构信息的能力。

Activity 4: Inferring feelings and emotions

本活动旨在落实课时目标3。

1. Read the text again and then discuss in pairs how Blackborow's feelings changed over time.

*Teacher can demonstrate the first and second boxes with students by asking the following questions.

Q1: In diary entry 1, how did Blackborow feel about himself before he joined the expedition?

Q2: Was he eager to join? How did you know?

Q3: Why did you say "confident"? What evidence can you find of his confidence?

Q4: While they were at sea, how did Blackborow feel? Any evidence?

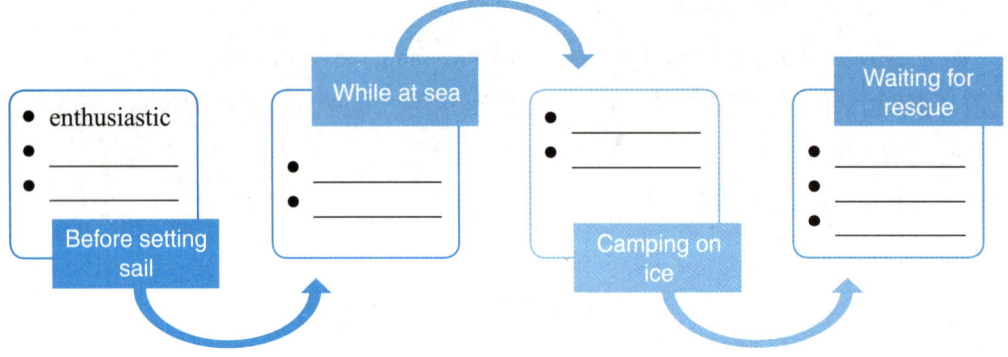

2. Discuss in pairs and then check the answers with the class.

【设计意图】引导学生再次深入阅读文本，小组讨论和分析主人公珀西心理状态的变化过程，学会依据事实作推断，促进思维能力向更高层次发展。

【核心素养提升点】培养学生依据事实作推断的思维习惯；提升学生的逻辑思维能力。

Assignment

1. Complete Activity 3 on page 40 of the Student Book.

2. Imagine you're Perce Blackborow. Write a message in a bottle of no less than 60 words. Here are some tips that may help you with your writing:

• use the first person perspective;

• describe your adversity, ask for help, or wish for a happy ending;

• use such expressions as join an expedition to, have to abandon, wait for rescue, get stuck, keep sb busy, hunt seal for food, have faith in, etc.

【设计意图】作业1中的文段是对前面阅读文本的大意概括，复现了话题词汇。该作业让学生根据上下文理解相关词义，阅读文段并完成填空，目的是考查学生的语言运用能力。作业2让学生以珀西的口吻写一封不少于60词的瓶中信，描述自己的遇险情况，发出求助信号或祈愿顺利。

【核心素养提升点】培养学生整合、概括文本信息的能力；提升学生的写作能力。

四、教学反思

本节课教学基本能达到预期的效果。在读前活动，学生能在教师一步步的引导下，积极调动已有知识，通过讨论图片、设计路线等活动感知南极探险的相关话题，储备如 Antarctica、penguin、adversity 等必要词汇。在读中活动，学生在快速浏览招募广告后能进一步预测南极探险存在的困难，为阅读和理解三则日记做铺垫。在阅读日记时，学生能够准确理解日记所描述的重要事件，然后以表格的形式梳理、归纳主要内容。此外，学生还能够对文本进行深层次分析，较好地推断和概括人物在历险过程中心理状态的变化，训练了逻辑思维能力。整节课真实呈现了在教师的递进式设计和耐心引导下，学生一步步走向深层次理解文本的过程。

本节课存在一些不足之处。一是由于学生的话题词汇储备不足，教师不得不花费较多时间处理 Antarctica 等必备的话题词汇；二是学生几乎没有深层次阅读文本的习惯，因此本节课活动推进较慢，原本该在课上完成的概要填空练习不得不改为课后完成。

第二课时

一、课时目标

1. 通过赏析优秀习作，学习和理解瓶中信的写作标准，积累、归类与话题相关的词汇，培养归纳、联想等学习策略。

2. 通过品读标题，尝试讨论和归纳人们面对逆境时所需要的品质；通过细读文本，分析和总结文本细节所反映的探险队主要人物的优秀品质。

3. 回归文本，通过角色扮演还原日记所记录的事件与情景，对文本内容和语言进行迁移运用，提升思维品质和语言能力。

二、设计思路

本节课基于第一课时的阅读成果进行设计，教学重点是深入分析文本细节所反映的人物品质。教师首先引导学生通过赏析优秀习作，激活背景知识，口头复习和巩固与话题相关的语言，从结构、内容和语言等方面归纳瓶中信的写作标准；接着引导学生品读标题，讨论标题的修辞手法和内在含义，分析谁是探险队全部生还的幕后功臣，尝试归纳人们面对逆境时所需要的品质；然后引导学生深入阅读文本，分析和总结文本细节所反映的主要人物品质；最后引导学生回归文本，分组进行角色扮演，还原日记所描述的重要事件过程，通过对话和肢体语言展现几位主要人物的性格特点，实现对文本内容和语言的迁移与运用，提升思维品质，锻炼语言表达能力。课后作业让学生围绕"最令人崇敬的探险队人物"这个话题进行写作，帮助学生巩固所学知识，培养学生坚毅的品质和乐观的精神。

三、教学过程

Activity 1: Reviewing the assignment

本活动旨在落实课时目标1。

1. Check the answers to the gap-filling exercise on page 40 of the Student Book.

2. Review and give comments on two students' assignments about the message in a bottle.

Q1: Do they relate to the theme of adversity, perseverance, and courage?

Q2: Were they written in the first person perspective?

Q3: Do the writers use words and expressions that relate to the theme?

Q4: Is there an ending such as looking forward to a rescue, or a farewell to life?

Q5: Do the writers display decent grammar and language use?

【设计意图】引导学生通过赏析和评价优秀习作，把握瓶中信的写作标准，反思自己的习作在内容与结构上是否合理，同时积累和归类与话题相关的词汇。

【核心素养提升点】培养学生交流和评价学习成果的能力。

Activity 2: Appreciating the title

本活动旨在落实课时目标2。

Read aloud the title and answer the questions.

Q1: What figure of speech is it?

Q2: What did they succeed in doing and what did they fail to do?

Q3: Is it a good title? Why or why not?

【设计意图】引导学生研读标题，通过分析两种不同的语言表达，如 successful（success）与 failure、safe return of all crew members 与 not reaching Antarctica 等，探究标题采用的修辞手法（Oxymoron 矛盾修辞法），挖掘标题内涵，为后面深入理解文本、分析主要人物的品质做好铺垫。

【核心素养提升点】提升学生的语言赏析能力；提升学生的逻辑思维能力。

Activity 3: Analysing behaviours and qualities

本活动旨在落实课时目标2。

1. Discuss and answer the question.

Q: Who could have contributed to the safe return of all crew members?

2. Discuss and list the qualities.

Q: What qualities are needed in the face of adversity?

3. Carefully read the following sentences from the three diary entries and infer what the behaviours say about the characters.

Diary entry 1:

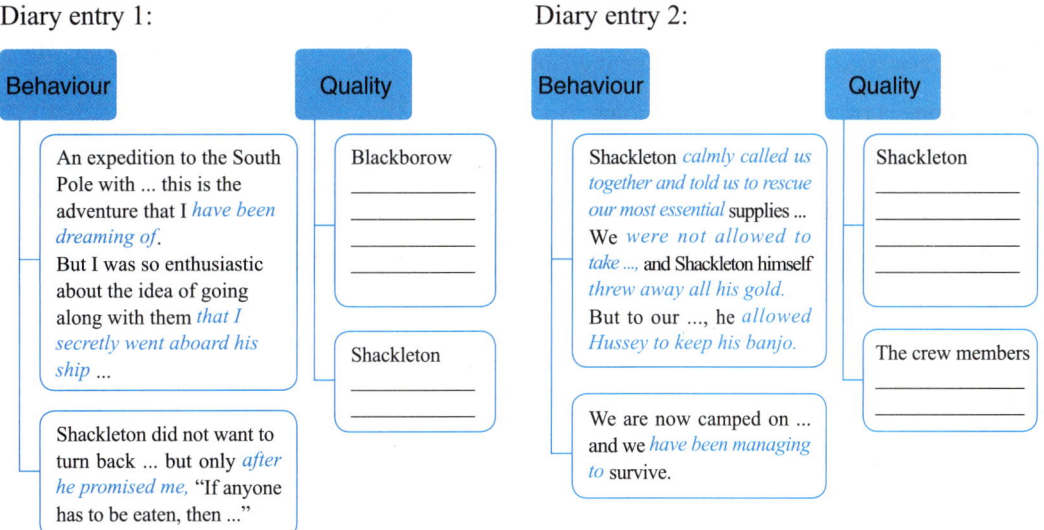

Diary entry 2:

Diary entry 3:

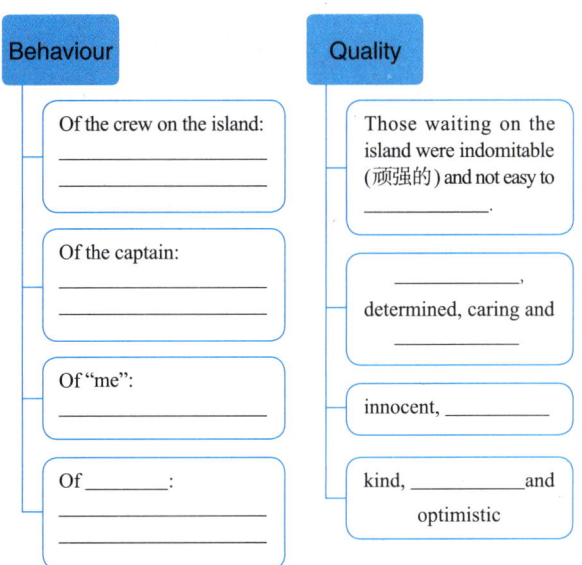

【设计意图】步骤1引导学生通过讨论，明白探险队最终得以全员生还，靠的是所有人的共同努力。步骤2让学生分组讨论，列举人们面对逆境时应具备的品质（形容词），如persevering、determined、calm、optimistic、confident、courageous、brave、ambitious等，为下一步分析人物品质做好铺垫。步骤3引导学生回归文本，分析和提炼文本细节所反映的人物品质。

【核心素养提升点】提升学生深层次理解文本的能力；培养学生的概括和评价能力；培养学生的优秀品格。

Activity 4: Doing role-plays

本活动旨在落实课时目标3。

In groups, prepare and act out a scene from the diary entries.

Criteria for a good scene include:

- the play has leading roles, supporting roles, and a narrator;
- actors/actresses use vivid and authentic language;
- the scene is two to three minutes long.

【设计意图】引导学生再次回归文本，分组进行角色扮演，在指定的时间内还原日记所记录的不同事件与情景。

【核心素养提升点】培养学生重组信息的能力；提升学生的综合语言运用能力；提升学生的思维品质。

Assignment

Write 80 words or more to explain which person in the text you admire the most.

Tips:

- use at least five newly learnt adjectives to describe the person;
- support your choice with evidence.

【设计意图】让学生以"最令人崇敬的探险队人物"为话题进行写作，帮助学生巩固语言知识，体会文本所传达的在面对逆境时应具备的勇气和品质，学会正视困难，以坚毅的品质和乐观的精神面对人生的逆境和挫折。

【核心素养提升点】培养学生的逻辑思维能力；提升学生的写作能力；培养学生的优秀品格和乐观精神。

四、教学反思

本节课总体上教学目标达成情况较好。首先，教师现场批改和点评部分习作，学生观摩优秀的作品，明确瓶中信写作的主题、结构、内容和语言特点。教师将部分习作呈现在学案中，作为参考范本供学生阅读与赏析。接着，学生开展深层次文本阅读，先赏析标题，进而讨论和分析日记中所呈现的细节及其所反映的人物性格与品质。学生能够较准确地推断"坚忍号"探险队主要人物的性格，并尝试归纳人们面对逆境时应具备的重要品质。

本节课存在一些不足之处。一方面，由于学生缺少深层次文本分析的常规训练，且词汇量相对有限，在分析人物品质这个环节，教师不敢放手让学生进行自主分析和提炼。教师干预较多，而且耗费了较多时间。另一方面，在最后的角色扮演环节，因时间有些仓促，学生对文本内容缺乏充分的理解，最后只有两位学生勇敢接受展示任务。尽管两位学生比较准确地展现了沙克尔顿和珀西的性格特点，但使用的语言比较苍白。教师可以在活动前提供必要的语言支架，以帮助学生更自信地进行表达。

第三节　提高版教学案例

教学内容安排：第一课时引导学生整体阅读文本，梳理关键信息，培养思维能力；第二课时引导学生赏析优秀习作，深化文本理解，加强协作训练，培养高阶思维能力和综合语言运用能力。

第一课时

一、课时目标

1. 通过讨论南极旅游相关话题，激活背景知识和相关话题语言；基于探究式学习模式阅读和理解招募广告，预测文本内容。
2. 运用寻读和略读的策略，进行无干扰阅读，自主梳理和提取文本关键信息。
3. 整合文本信息，分析描述情绪变化的语言，自主推断人物心理状态的变化，提升逻辑思维能力和批判性思维能力。

二、设计思路

本节课的重点是梳理文本信息。教师在激活学生与南极探险有关的背景知识和话题语言的基础上，引导学生理解和提取关键信息。教师首先通过一则名言，引导学生讨论南极旅游相关内容，由此导入本节课话题，激发学生的阅读兴趣；接着让学生阅读招募广告，以问题"If there was an article about this journey, what information would you expect to read about?"鼓励学生大胆预测文本内容；之后让学生寻读文本，以表格或其他形式自主提取关键信息；然后引导学生略读三则日记，通过"when—where—what"的表格模式梳理和归纳信息；最后带领学生深入解读文本，通过分析主人公在探险不同阶段的情绪变化，推断其心理状态的变化。本节课的课后作业是以珀西的口吻写一封瓶中信，为第二课时的写作微技能训练做好铺垫。

三、教学过程

Activity 1: Talking about travelling to Antarctica

本活动旨在落实课时目标1。

Consider this quote: "The world is a book and those who do not travel read only one page." Now answer the questions.

Q1: When is the best time for us to go to Antarctica?

Q2: How can we go there?

Q3: What can we do there?

【设计意图】通过引用名言导入关于南极旅游的话题，并引导学生讨论三个相关问题，激活学生关于南极洲的背景知识，引出penguin、bitter cold、long months of darkness、ice-breaker、the southern hemisphere、aurora等话题词汇，为学生预测文本内容及深入理解探险队遇到的困难做好铺垫。

【核心素养提升点】提升学生围绕文本主题进行口头表达的能力；提升学生的发散性思维能力。

Activity 2: Inquiring about the advertisement to predict the content of the text

本活动旨在落实课时目标1。

Look through the advertisement and answer the following questions.

Q1: What information can you get?

Q2: Will you apply if you are seeking a job?

Q3: If there was an article about this journey, what information would you expect to read about?

【设计意图】引导学生带着对南极洲的兴趣阅读沙克尔顿的招募广告，开展探究式学习，提出自己想要从文中获取的信息，借此预测文本内容，主动聚焦主题语境。

【核心素养提升点】提升学生预测文本内容的能力；培养学生自主探究的能力。

Activity 3: Identifying the key information of the expedition

本活动旨在落实课时目标2。

1. Scan Paragraph 1 to find out the key information of the text.

Who	Perce Blackborow, Sir Ernest Shackleton, other crew members
What	an expedition
Where	Antarctica
When	from 1914 to 1916
How	by sea (on the ship *Endurance*)
Why	to explore the unknown

2. Skim the three diary entries to find out the "where" and "what" of each with a limit of 8 words.

When	Where	What
31 Oct 1914	at sea	"I" joined the expedition.
21 Nov 1915	on floating ice	"We" got stuck and abandoned the ship.
20 May 1916	on Elephant Island	Waiting for rescue, "we" struggled to survive.

【设计意图】引导学生运用寻读和略读的策略，分别对文本的首段以及三则日记进行无干扰阅读。步骤1引导学生对文本所描述的南极探险历程做整体的信息梳理。步骤2引导学生整体阅读三则日记，概括每则日记所描述的主要事件，一方面可以提升学生的归纳和概括能

力；另一方面可以引导学生理解探险队所经历的磨难，为下一个活动，即梳理主人公心理状态的变化做好铺垫。

【核心素养提升点】培养学生整理和概括文本信息的能力。

Activity 4: Inferring feelings and emotions

本活动旨在落实课时目标3。

1. Read the text again and discuss in groups how Blackborow's feelings changed over time.

Q1: What are the four stages of Blackborow's journey?

Q2: Are there any useful words or expressions in the diary entries that help you to tell what Blackborow's feelings were?

2. Draw a flowchart to help you explain.

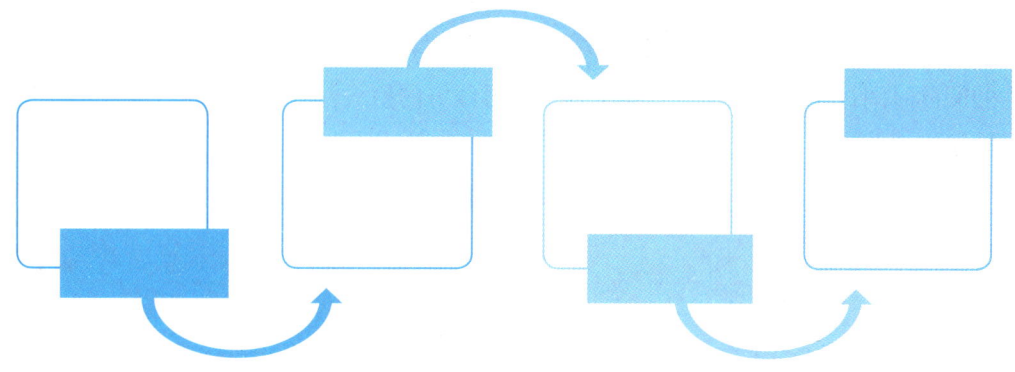

3. Present answers and explain them.

【设计意图】引导学生依据事实作推断，小组讨论并梳理主人公的心理状态一共经历了哪几个阶段，即：出海前的满腔热情、急于表现和充满自信，出海后得到沙克尔顿同意留在船上时的兴奋和骄傲，弃船扎营浮冰上时的低落和担忧，最后在象岛等候救援时的忧虑、茫然却又心存希望。

【核心素养提升点】培养学生分析、概括和整合信息的能力；提升学生的逻辑思维能力和批判性思维能力。

Assignment

Imagine you're Perce Blackborow. Write a message in a bottle of no less than 80 words. Here are some tips that may help you with your writing:

- use the first person perspective;
- describe your adversity, ask for help, or wish for a happy ending;
- use expressions newly learnt today.

【设计意图】要求学生根据写作建议，以珀西的口吻写一封不少于80词的瓶中信，描述自己所处的困境，并发出求助信号或者祈愿顺利。

【核心素养提升点】培养学生概括和整合文本信息的能力；提升学生的综合语言运用能力。

四、教学反思

本节课的教学目标达成度较高，学生积极参与课堂活动，表现符合预期。本节课教学活动多样，既有对浅层信息的处理，如讨论招募广告的主要内容，找寻事件发生的时间、地点、人物等细节信息，也包含了对深层信息的挖掘，如用不超过八个词概括事件、推断人物心理状态的变化等。教师在教学时，既提供了阅读策略的指导，也有写作手法的点拨。结合文本内容设计的南极旅游话题问题链，既能引出目标语言，又能加深学生对话题词汇及文本内容的理解。此外，教学活动形式也较为多样。以概括人物在历险过程中情绪和心理状态的变化为例，学生分析珀西心理状态的变化，并指出不同的心理状态所对应的场合。这个过程对学生的思维能力以及语言概括和运用能力有着较高的要求。对于程度较好的学生，这个活动形式激发了他们的学习兴趣，也锻炼了他们深度学习、自主学习和合作学习的能力，有效地促进了学生思维品质的发展。

本节课存在一些不足之处。例如，教师的反馈语偶有失误。再如，活动3的第一个任务留给学生的阅读时间过长，部分学生感受不到该学习任务的挑战性，导致课堂气氛有些沉闷。

第二课时

一、课时目标

1. 通过赏析优秀习作，自主归纳瓶中信的写作标准，积累、归类与话题相关的词汇，培养归纳、联想等学习策略。
2. 研读标题，自主探究标题采用的修辞手法，挖掘标题内涵；深入解读文本，根据探险队主要人物的言行推断和总结他们的优秀品质。
3. 描述自己敬佩的人物并讲述原因，提升口头表达能力和思辨能力；进行独立写作，描述自己曾经或正在面对的逆境，提升书面表达能力和思维品质。

二、设计思路

本节课基于第一课时的阅读成果进行设计，注重引导学生挖掘和解读文本深层信息。教师首先引导学生通过赏析优秀习作，自主归纳瓶中信的写作标准；接着引导学生研读标题，自主探究标题采用的修辞手法，探讨标题的内在含义，为后面推断和总结主要人物品质做铺垫；然后引导学生深入阅读文本，分析描述不同人物行为的句子，并根据沙克尔顿、珀西等主要人物的言行推断和总结他们的优秀品质；最后引导学生完成口头表达活动以及写作活动。口头表达活动是在沙克尔顿和珀西之间选择一位自己更敬佩的人，并阐述自己敬佩他的原因。写作活动是描述自己曾经或正在面临的逆境。本节课通过这些活动，一方面提升学生的综合语言运用能力和思维能力；另一方面帮助学生明确战胜困难需要坚毅的品质和乐观的精神，培养学生勇于面对挫折与逆境的强大心态。

三、教学过程

Activity 1: Reviewing the assignment

本活动旨在落实课时目标1。

Review and give comments on two students' assignments.

Q1: Do they relate to the theme of adversity, perseverance, and courage?

Q2: Were they written in the first person perspective?

Q3: Do the writers use words and expressions that relate to the theme?

【设计意图】引导学生通过赏析和评价优秀习作，自主探究和归纳瓶中信的写作标准，积累和归类与话题相关的词汇，反思自己的习作在内容与结构上是否合理。

【核心素养提升点】培养学生交流和评价学习成果的能力。

Activity 2: Appreciating the title

本活动旨在落实课时目标2。

Read aloud the title and answer the questions.

Q1: What figure of speech is it?

Q2: What did they succeed in doing and what did they fail to do?

Q3: Is it a good title? Why or why not?

【设计意图】引导学生研读标题，自主探究标题的特别之处，探讨标题中的"successful（success）"与"failure"分别可能指什么，分析这种修辞手法（Oxymoron 矛盾修辞法）的特点，即用两种不相调和的词语形容一件事，起到一种"令人意外的、引人入胜的"效果；引导学生通过挖掘标题内涵，重新领会成功和失败的定义，学会辩证地看待成败，为后面深入理解文本、分析主要人物的品质做好铺垫。

【核心素养提升点】提升学生的语言赏析能力；提升学生的逻辑思维能力。

Activity 3: Analysing behaviours and qualities

本活动旨在落实课时目标2。

1. Discuss and answer the question.

Q: Who could have contributed to the safe return of all crew members?

2. Discuss and list the qualities.

Q: What qualities are needed in the face of adversity?

3. Carefully read the following sentences from the three diary entries and infer what the behaviours say about the characters.

Diary entry 1:

An expedition to the South Pole with the great Sir Ernest Shackleton—this is the adventure that I have been dreaming of. Shackleton turned me down because he thought I was too young and wasn't qualified. But I was so enthusiastic about the idea of going along with them that I secretly went aboard his ship.

Shackleton did not want to turn back so he offered me a job, but only after he promised me, "If anyone has to be eaten, then you will be the first!"

Blackborow _____
_____
_____
_____
_____
_____
_____

Shackleton _____
_____
_____

Diary entry 2:

Shackleton calmly called us together and told us to rescue our most essential supplies—the small boats, our food, the cook stove, candles, clothes, and blankets. This was no time to panic. We were not allowed to take most of our personal belongings, and Shackleton himself threw away all his gold. But to our surprise, he allowed Hussey to keep his banjo.

We are now camped on the ice and we have been managing to survive, but spring is coming, and the ice will soon begin to melt.

Shackleton _____
_____
_____
_____
_____
_____
_____

The crew members _____
_____
_____

Diary entry 3:

Of the crew on the island:
_____

Of the captain:
_____

Of "me":
_____

Of _____:
_____

Those waiting on the island _____
_____
_____
_____
_____

UNIT 4 ADVERSITY AND COURAGE

【设计意图】步骤1引导学生通过讨论，明白探险队最终得以全员生还，靠的是所有人的共同努力，以此锻炼学生的批判性思维能力。步骤2让学生分组讨论，列举人们面对逆境时应具备的品质（形容词）。步骤3引导学生回归文本，阅读和分析描述不同人物行为的句子，提炼与归纳其所反映的人物品质。

【核心素养提升点】提升学生赏析语言的能力；提升学生的逻辑思维能力和批判性思维能力；培养学生的优秀品格。

Activity 4: Discussing

本活动旨在落实课时目标3。

Choose the character you admire more and state your reasons.

Q: Which of the characters do you admire more, Perce Blackborow or Ernest Shackleton? Why?

【设计意图】引导学生描述自己更敬佩的人物并说明理由。

【核心素养提升点】提升学生表述个人观点的能力；提升学生的批判性思维能力。

Activity 5: Writing

本活动旨在落实课时目标3。

1. Write about a difficult situation that you have faced or are facing now. Describe the difficulty and specify how you overcame or will overcome it.

2. Compare essays with partner and share ideas.

【设计意图】让学生独立写作，描述一个自己曾经或正在面对的逆境，以及具体（将）如何战胜这个逆境，然后与同伴交换习作，相互交流学习。

【核心素养提升点】培养学生的综合语言运用能力；帮助学生养成与同伴交流学习成果的习惯。

Assignment

Complete and polish your writing.

【设计意图】让学生根据与同伴交流的心得体会，进一步完善自己的作品。

【核心素养提升点】培养学生虚心好学的品质；培养学生不断自我完善的意识。

四、教学反思

本节课总体上较好地达成了教学目标。在作业讲评环节，学生充分赏析了同伴的优秀作品，明确了瓶中信写作的主题、结构、内容和语言特点。学生通过问题链理解了探险队队员所具备的优秀品质是决定他们全部生还的关键因素。在此基础上，学生再次深入阅读文本，通过分析细节，挖掘、提炼和归纳探险队主要人物面对逆境时所具有的一系列重要品质。教师充分利用了教室的设施（实物投影仪），请学生现场展示他们在学案上写的关于优秀品质的词汇并做适度解说，一方面为学生提供了展示自我的平台，另一方面给全班学生向同伴学习的机会。最后，学生通过口头和书面两种形式的表达活动，进一步实现对文本内容和语言的迁移运用。整节课学生参与度高，在活动中不断探索和领悟文本所传递的内涵，即在逆境面前人们应具有顽强拼搏、坚韧不拔的精神。

同时，教师在一些环节处理得比较拖沓。例如，在活动1，学生交流瓶中信习作耗时较长。由于学生英语基础不错，教师不必在活动最后再花时间为学生呈现与话题相关的词汇。再如，在活动3，列举品质这个环节耗费了较多时间，影响了整体课堂效率。

UNIT 5 POEMS
Reading and Thinking   A FEW SIMPLE FORMS OF ENGLISH POEMS

第一节　文本解读

一、总体解读

本单元的主题是"诗歌"。阅读文本"A Few Simple Forms of English Poems"通过介绍几种简单的诗歌形式，在帮助学生了解诗歌的基本特征与语言特点的同时，培养学生对诗歌的赏析能力以及审美情趣，并引导学生尝试进行简单的诗歌创作。学生在学习活动中理解和欣赏诗歌语言的形式美，并从作品的主题内涵中了解诗人表达的思想情感，获得积极的人生启示。

该文本是一篇说明文。作者先简述了诗人们创作诗歌的原因以及诗歌这一类体裁的基本特点，接着重点介绍了五种比较简单的诗歌形式。全文共七段，篇章结构为"总—分—总"。第一段概述了诗人进行诗歌创作的原因，并从诗歌的语言形式、内容及意义等方面介绍了诗歌这种文学体裁的特点，然后引出下文；第二至第六段分别介绍了童谣、清单诗、五行诗、俳句和唐诗五种诗歌形式，并根据五种诗歌的主要特点进行举例说明；第七段简单收尾，鼓励读者尝试用英语进行诗歌创作。

在阅读策略方面，教师可以引导学生了解说明文的脉络结构；引导学生寻找关键词，利用图表归纳、整合零散的信息点；帮助学生理解举例子、下定义等主要的说明方法；最后引导学生利用从文本中提炼出来的欣赏诗歌的维度指导诗歌赏析和创作，提升读写能力。

二、段落解读

表1：分段解读

The original text	Interpretation
A FEW SIMPLE FORMS OF ENGLISH POEMS	1. What is the text type? Exposition. 2. According to the title, six poems, and pictures, what do you think the text is about?

续表

The original text	Interpretation
	It is an introduction to a few simple forms of English poems. **3. Why does the writer provide the six poems?** To serve as examples to illustrate the characteristics of different forms of English poems. **4. Who may be the intended readers of this text? Why?** Perhaps English poetry beginners, as the text only introduces some simple forms of poetry.
There are various reasons why people compose poetry. Some poems tell a story or describe a certain image in the reader's mind. Others try to convey certain feelings such as joy and sorrow. The distinctive characteristics of poetry often include economical use of words, descriptive and vivid language, integrated imagery, literary devices such as similes and metaphors, and arrangement of words, lines, rhymes, and rhythm. Poets use many different forms of poetry to express themselves. Now we will look at a few of the simpler forms.	**1. Why do people compose poetry?** To tell a story or describe a certain image in the poet's mind, or to convey certain feelings. Basically, to express themselves. **2. What are the distinctive characteristics of poetry?** The distinctive characteristics of poetry often include economical use of words, descriptive and vivid language, integrated imagery, literary devices, and arrangement of words, lines, rhymes, and rhythm. **3. What categories can the characteristics be put into?** (1) format: arrangement of words, lines, rhymes, and rhythm; (2) sound: rhyme, syllable, rhythm; (3) language: economical use of words, descriptive and vivid language, literary devices; (4) image/picture: integrated imagery; (5) message/feeling: Poets use many different forms of poetry to express themselves. **4. What is the purpose of this paragraph?** To give readers a brief introduction to English poetry and state some aspects from which a poem is appreciated. **5. What is the function of the last sentence in this paragraph?** To serve as the transitional sentence for the following content.

The original text	Interpretation
Some of the first poems a young child learns in English are nursery rhymes. They are usually the traditional poems or folk songs. The language of these rhymes, like Poem A, is to the point but has a storyline. Many children enjoy nursery rhymes because they rhyme, have a strong rhythm, and often repeat the same words. The poems may not make sense and even seem contradictory, but they are easy to learn and recite. By playing with the words in nursery rhymes, children learn about language. **A** Hush, little baby, don't say a word, Papa's gonna buy you a mockingbird. If that mockingbird won't sing, Papa's gonna buy you a diamond ring. If that diamond ring turns to brass, Papa's gonna buy you a looking glass. If that looking glass gets broke, Papa's gonna buy you a billy goat. If that billy goat won't pull, Papa's gonna buy you a cart and bull.	**1. What is the function of the first sentence in this paragraph?** To introduce the topic of this paragraph. **2. What form of poetry is introduced in this paragraph?** The nursery rhyme. **3. What are the characteristics of nursery rhymes?** The language of nursery rhymes is to the point but has a storyline. They rhyme, have a strong rhythm, repeat words, may not make sense, and even seem contradictory. **4. Which words in this paragraph show the accuracy of exposition language?** Some, usually, many, often, may not. **5. Why do nursery rhymes have such characteristics?** The poems are intended for children who can learn about language by playing with the words. The last sentence often echoes the first sentence. **6. What are the features of Poem A?** Subject/topic: Papa's words to put his baby to sleep Sound: (1) rhyme (word—bird; sing—ring; brass—glass; broke—goat; pull—bull); (2) strong rhythm; (3) mockingbird, diamond ring, looking glass, billy goat, and cart and bull all contain three syllables. Language: literary device—repetition Feeling: Papa's deep love for his baby

The original text	Interpretation
One of the simplest kinds of poem is the "list poem", which contains a list of things, people, ideas, or descriptions that develop a particular theme. List poems have a flexible line length and repeated phrases which give both a pattern and a rhythm to the poem. Some rhyme [like B and C], while others do not. **B** Only One Mother Hundreds of stars in the pretty sky, Hundreds of shells on the shore together, Hundreds of birds that go singing by, Hundreds of lambs in the sunny weather. Hundreds of dewdrops to greet the dawn, Hundreds of bees in the purple clover, Hundreds of butterflies on the lawn, But only one mother the wide world over. *George Cooper* **C** LIFE Life can be good, Life can be bad, Life is mostly cheerful, But sometimes sad. Life can be dreams, Life can be great thoughts, Life can mean a person, Sitting in court.	**1. What form of poetry is introduced in this paragraph?** The list poem. **2. What are the characteristics of list poems?** They contain a list of things, people, ideas, or descriptions that develop a particular theme; they have a flexible line length; they have repeated phrases which give both a pattern and a rhythm to the poem; some rhyme while others do not. **3. What are the features of Poem B?** Subject/topic: Mother Sound: (1) rhyme (sky—by; together—weather; dawn—lawn; clover—over); (2) strong rhythm Language: literary devices (repetition, personification, contrast) "Hundreds of" is repeated to stress the large number of things, and "only one mother" is used in contrast to emphasise the value of a mother. Image/picture: Stars in the pretty sky, shells on the shore, flying singing birds, lambs in the sunny weather, dewdrops at dawn, bees in the purple clover, butterflies on the lawn. All these are beautiful and colourful natural sights. Feeling: love for one's mother **4. What are the features of Poem C?** Subject/topic: life Language: Repetition is used to give the poem a pattern; a list of adjectives and important things in life are used to make a contrast. Message: Life is full of possibilities and it's up to you to decide what your life will be like. Try to make it better.

续表

The original text	Interpretation
Another simple form of poem that amateurs can easily write is the *cinquain*, which is made up of five lines. With these, you can convey a strong picture or a certain mood in just a few words. Look at the example [D]. **D** Brother Beautiful, athletic Teasing, shouting, laughing Friend and enemy too Mine	**1. What form of poetry is introduced in this paragraph?** The *cinquain*. **2. What are the characteristics of the *cinquain*?** It is made up of five lines and conveys a strong picture or a certain mood in just a few words. **3. What picture and mood does Poem D convey?** It conveys a strong picture of a good-looking, naughty, noisy, and energetic brother. It expresses the feeling that the writer loves his/her brother and is proud of having such a brother, although sometimes he/she may be unhappy about his naughtiness. **4. What is the function of each line in a *cinquain*?** Line 1: one-word subject; Line 2: two adjectives that describe the subject; Line 3: three verbs ending in "*-ing*" that describe actions relating to the subject; Line 4: a four-word phrase that describes a feeling relating to the subject; Line 5: one specific word that refers back to Line 1.
Haiku is a Japanese form of poetry that consists of 17 syllables. It has a format of three lines, containing 5, 7, and 5 syllables respectively. It is not a traditional form of English poetry, but is very popular with English writers. It is easy to write and, like the *cinquain*, can give a clear picture and create a special feeling using very few words. The *haiku* poem [E] on the right is a translation from Japanese, which shows a moment in the life of a delicate butterfly. **E** A fallen blossom Is coming back to the branch. Look, a butterfly!	**1. What form of poetry is introduced in this paragraph?** *Haiku*. **2. What are the characteristics of a *haiku* poem?** It has a format of three lines, containing 5, 7, 5 syllables respectively; it gives a clear picture and creates a special feeling. **3. What is the syllable pattern of Poem E?** A fall-en blos-som Is com-ing back to the branch. Look, a but-ter-fly! **4. What picture and feeling does the poem convey?** A butterfly, which looks like a blossom, flies up and rests on a branch. The poem shows the writer's amazement, and admiration for the beauty of nature.

The original text	Interpretation
English speakers also enjoy poems from China, those from the Tang Dynasty in particular. A lot of Tang poetry has been translated into English, such as this one [F]. **F** Where she awaits her husband On and on the river flows. Never looking back, Transformed into stone. Day by day upon the mountain top, wind and rain revolve. Should the traveller return, this stone would utter speech. *Wang Jian*	**1. What is the original Chinese version of Poem F?** 望夫石 　　（唐）王建 望夫处，江悠悠， 化为石，不回头。 山头日日风复雨， 行人归来石应语。 **2. What would the stone wife say to her husband if he came back?** (Answers may vary.) You are finally home. I missed you so much. Where have you been all these years? Have you been well these years? ... **3. What feelings of the poet are conveyed in the poem?** He had strong sympathy and admiration for those women whose husbands were far away, and he sang high praise for their unfailing love. **4. What are the features of the poem?** Subject/topic: a stone wife Language: literary device—personification Phrases like "on and on" and "day by day" are used to stress the long distance and long time. Image/picture: It conveys a picture that a stone wife is standing on top of a mountain, staring at a river and waiting for her husband to come back. Feeling: great sympathy and admiration for those loyal and faithful wives
With so many different forms of poetry to choose from, you may eventually want to write poems of your own. Give it a try!	**1. What is the function of this paragraph?** To end the text with a strong message to encourage the readers to try writing a poem themselves. **2. What does "it" refer to in the last sentence?** To write poems of your own.

表2：跨段解读

Putting it all together

1. How would you describe the three parts of the text?
The first part is the leading part, which introduces the main topic—a few simple forms of English poems; the second part illustrates the characteristics of five simple forms of English poems; the third part brings the text to an end.

2. What forms of simple poems are introduced in the text?
Nursery rhyme, list poem, *cinquain*, *haiku*, and Tang poem.

3. What expository techniques are mainly used in the text?
Giving definitions and examples.

4. From what aspects can an English poem be appreciated?
(1) format; (2) subject/topic; (3) sound; (4) language; (5) image/picture; (6) message/feeling (theme)

5. What are the main steps of writing an English poem?
(1) Decide on a subject/topic and make sure what message or feeling you want to convey.
(2) Choose a form of poetry and think of the format required, if necessary.
(3) Think about the words, phrases, and literary devices you would like to use. Make it rhyme and give it a rhythm if you want.
(4) See how well the details paint a picture in your head, and write down the image you see.
(5) Read it aloud to yourself or your friends and make some improvements.

三、综合解读

综合上述分析，我们对文本进行教学设计时，应着重考量以下三个方面。

1. 语言学习

本单元阅读文本的语言学习可围绕"Introducing and appreciating a few simple forms of English poems"展开。教师可引导学生梳理与话题相关的词汇，如distinctive characteristics、format、theme、rhyme、syllable、rhythm、literary devices、integrated imagery、mood等名词或名词短语，以及have a strong rhythm、be made up of、contain、consist of、convey a strong picture、give a clear picture、convey a certain mood、create a special feeling等动词或动词短语。教师应引导学生关注在说明文中体现语言准确性的词汇，如some、usually、many、often、may等。此外，赏析诗歌语言也十分重要。教师应引导学生体会诗歌语言简洁、凝练、生动的特点，识别诗歌中运用的修辞手法。

2. 思维培养

在进行思维培养教学设计时，教师可围绕"sorting out the aspects from which an English poem is appreciated → appreciating example poems from the aspects → composing simple poems"这条主线

展开，首先引导学生将解释性文字与对应的诗歌例子结合起来进行对照阅读，感受举例子、下定义等常见说明方法的运用，深入了解诗歌的特点；然后引导学生用整理出来的诗歌赏析视角，尝试对五首诗歌进行赏析，体会诗歌的"形式美、音韵美、意象美、意义美"，领会诗歌创作的价值；最后鼓励学生尝试自己创作英语诗歌，培养批判性思维能力和创造性思维能力。

3. 文化意识

英语诗歌是西方文学的重要组成部分。教师要引导学生通过对文本的解读，理解诗歌是通过形象思维，用凝练、生动、诉诸感官、富有声音美的语言，反映现实生活，传递作者观点态度，抒发作者思想感情的一种文学体裁。教师不仅要引导学生体会英语诗歌形式上的美，也要引导学生分析诗歌所承载的文化内涵，发现诗歌意义上的美，体会其所传递的积极的人生观和价值观。教师可以引导学生重点关注和探讨诗歌中作者要传递的对于亲情、友情、爱情、大自然等的情感和对生活的感悟，培养学生的审美情趣，激发他们对生活的热爱。

第二节　通用版教学案例

教学内容安排：第一课时引导学生在感知全文概貌的基础上，重点阅读文本第一至第三段，学会赏析相应诗例；第二课时引导学生重点阅读文本第四至第七段，赏析相应诗例并将打乱的诗句组合成诗。

第一课时

一、课时目标

1. 通过阅读介绍性文字，理解与诗歌有关的重要词汇的含义，提炼诗歌赏析的几个主要维度，提升分类概括能力。
2. 通过快速阅读，获取文本基本信息，梳理文本结构，了解举例子的说明方法。
3. 通过诗歌阅读感受童谣的特点，利用归纳出来的赏析维度赏析童谣诗例，锻炼赏析能力；在文本阅读中定位核心信息，训练信息提取能力。
4. 利用所学词汇和诗歌赏析的几个维度，赏析文本中的清单诗，体会清单诗的特点，并结合语言分析，深入理解诗意。

二、设计思路

本节课围绕理解重点词汇、梳理文本结构、归纳诗歌赏析维度并将其用于诗例赏析这几个活动展开。教师首先用《一闪一闪小星星》这首学生非常熟悉的童谣引入话题，介绍诗歌的部分基本要素，解释较难的词汇，为诗例赏析做好铺垫；接着引导学生识别文体，阅读文本第一段，找出该段的两个关键词（reasons 和 characteristics）并定位支撑这两个关键词的细节信息，从形式、内容和意义三个方面归纳诗歌赏析的六个维度，即 format、subject/topic、sound、language、image/picture、message/feeling（theme）；随后让学生快速阅读文本，判断文本介绍的主要诗歌形式，识别作者运用的最主要的说明方法——举例子，梳理篇章脉络，画出文本结构图；然后鼓励学生在不看说明性文字的情况下自主赏析诗例A，再将自己的赏析和说明性文字进行比较，加深对童谣的理解；最后引导学生细读第三段，归纳清单诗的特征，完善文本结构图并通过自主提问赏析诗例，思考诗例传达的思想感情，巩固所学的赏析技能和词汇。

三、教学过程

Activity 1: Activating background knowledge related to poems

本活动为实现课时目标1和课时目标2做铺垫。

1. Read *Twinkle, Twinkle, Little Star* together. Sing along if possible, and then answer some questions.

Twinkle, twinkle, little star,

How I wonder what you are!

Up above the world so high,

Like a diamond in the sky.

Q1: What is the subject/topic of the song?

(A star.)

Q2: Read the last word of each line. What are they?

(They are rhyming words.)

2. Read and clap on each syllable.

Q: How many syllables are there in each line?

(Seven.)

T: They all have the same number of syllables, which gives the poem a strong rhythm. Rhyme, syllable, and rhythm make the sound of a poem.

3. Identify the literary devices in this poem.

Q1: The poet uses various literary devices. What literary device is used in the last sentence – "Like a diamond in the sky." ?

(Simile.)

Q2: Do you know any other literary devices?

(Metaphor, repetition, contrast, personification, etc.)

【设计意图】引导学生朗诵《一闪一闪小星星》这首童谣，激发学习兴趣，激活与英语诗歌有关的背景知识，同时了解英语诗歌的部分基本特点和赏析维度，包括subject/topic 和 sound（rhyme、syllable、rhythm）；引导学生对理解可能有困难的新词汇进行重点学习，如 rhyme、syllable、rhythm、literary device 等，并对 literary device 进行适当拓展，为后面阅读活动做好词汇上的准备。

【核心素养提升点】帮助学生进一步理解英语诗歌的韵律和节奏。

Activity 2: Predicting the text type and noting the aspects of poem appreciation

本活动旨在落实课时目标1。

1. Predict the text type by looking at the title.

(Exposition.)

2. Read the first paragraph, locate two key words, and answer the following questions.

Q1: What is the first key word?

(Reasons.)

Q2: What are the reasons why people compose poetry?

(Some poems tell a story or describe a certain image in the reader's mind. Others try to convey certain feelings such as joy and sorrow.)

T: Basically, they write poems to "express themselves", which means to convey a message or a certain feeling.

Q3: What is the second key word?

(Characteristics.)

Q4: What are the characteristics of English poetry?

(The distinctive characteristics of English poetry often include economical use of words, descriptive and vivid language, integrated imagery, literary devices such as similes and metaphors, and arrangement of words, lines, rhymes, and rhythm.)

3. **Note the aspects from which an English poem is appreciated.**

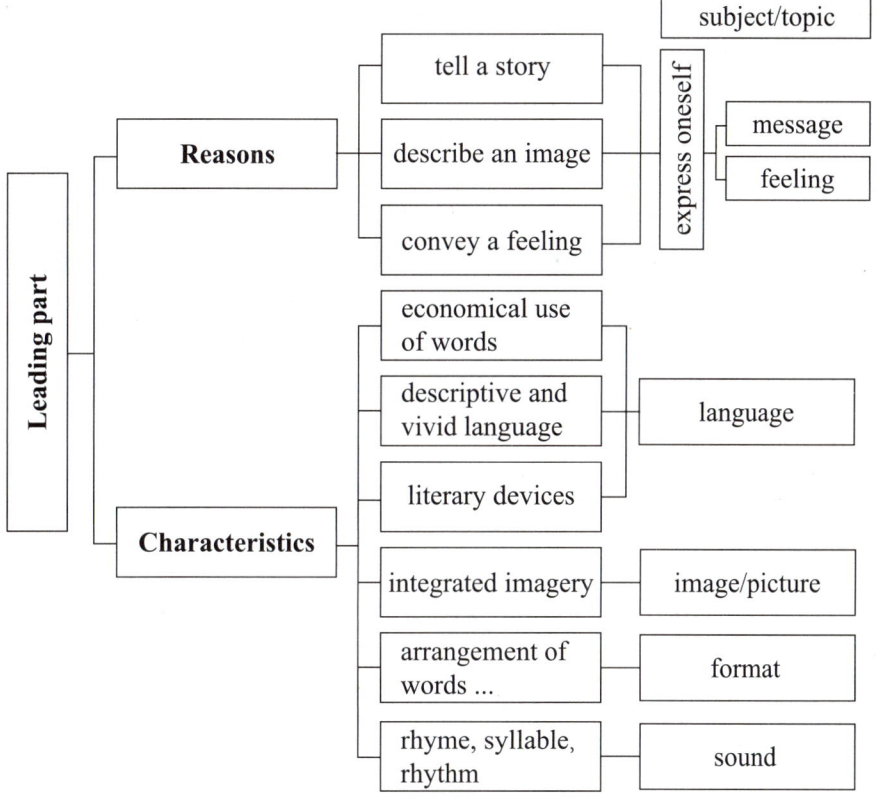

Aspects of poem appreciation	Form	format
	Content	subject/topic
		sound language image/picture
	Meaning	message/feeling (theme)

4. **Read the last sentence of the paragraph and figure out the function of it.**

【设计意图】步骤1让学生根据文本标题预测文体,旨在培养学生的文体意识,锻炼学生的预测能力,同时为后面引导学生关注文本中举例子等说明方法做铺垫。步骤2引导学生先快速阅读首段,找出该段中的两个关键词(reasons和characteristics),然后通过回答问题,提取重要细节信息,在阅读过程中归纳诗歌赏析的几大维度。步骤3引导学生结合读前活动中所引入的两个维度(subject/topic、sound),总结完整的诗歌赏析六维度。步骤4引导学生思考段末句承上启下的功能,关注form一词,为下文赏析几种不同形式的诗歌做铺垫。

【核心素养提升点】培养学生主动思考的能力;提升学生合理预测的能力;提升学生查找、提取、整合关键信息的能力。

Activity 3: Drawing the structure of the text

本活动旨在落实课时目标2。

1. Find the forms of English poems which are introduced in the text.

Q1: How many paragraphs are there in the text?

Q2: How many forms are introduced? What are they?

(Five forms: nursery rhyme, list poem, *cinquain*, *haiku*, and Tang poem.)

2. Find the main expository technique in this text.

Q: What technique would you use if you were going to introduce or explain something to others?

(Giving examples.)

3. Match the forms of poetry with the example poems and show the structure of the text.

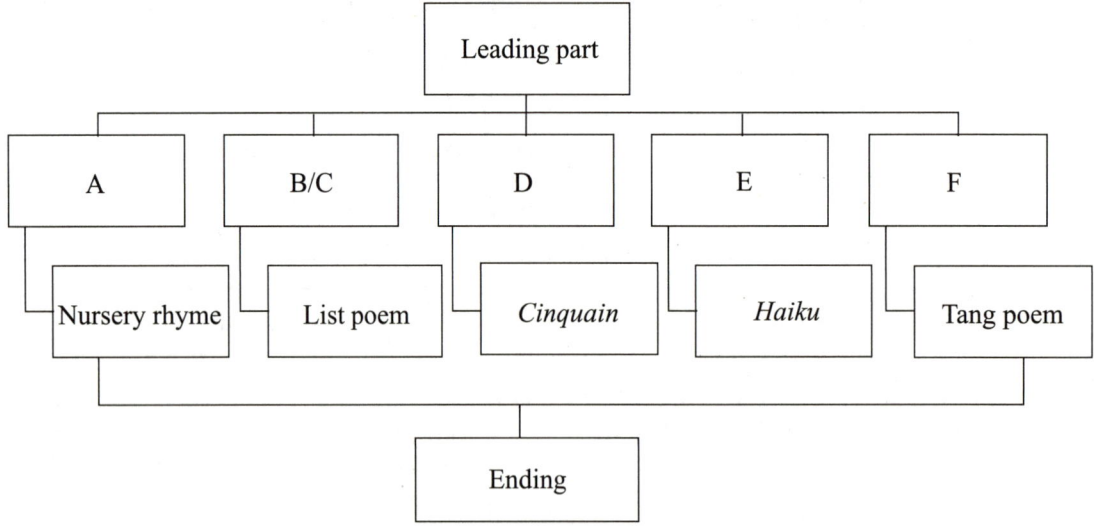

【设计意图】引导学生根据每段首句,快速找到文本所涉及的几种诗歌形式,将诗歌形式与对应的诗例配对,绘制文本结构图,同时感受举例子这一说明方法在说明文中的作用。

【核心素养提升点】提升学生的逻辑思维能力;培养学生在快速阅读中查找重要信息的能力;提升学生梳理文本结构的能力。

Activity 4: Learning about the nursery rhyme

本活动旨在落实课时目标3。

1. Read Poem A and clap the rhythm.

T: Read Poem A without referring to the introduction part on the left. Read the poem together and clap the rhythm.

2. Appreciate Poem A from the appreciation aspects.

T: Talk with a partner about Poem A and then share your ideas about the poem's appreciation aspects. Pay attention: format is not a distinctive characteristic of nursery rhymes.

3. Match the appreciation aspects with the characteristics of the poem.

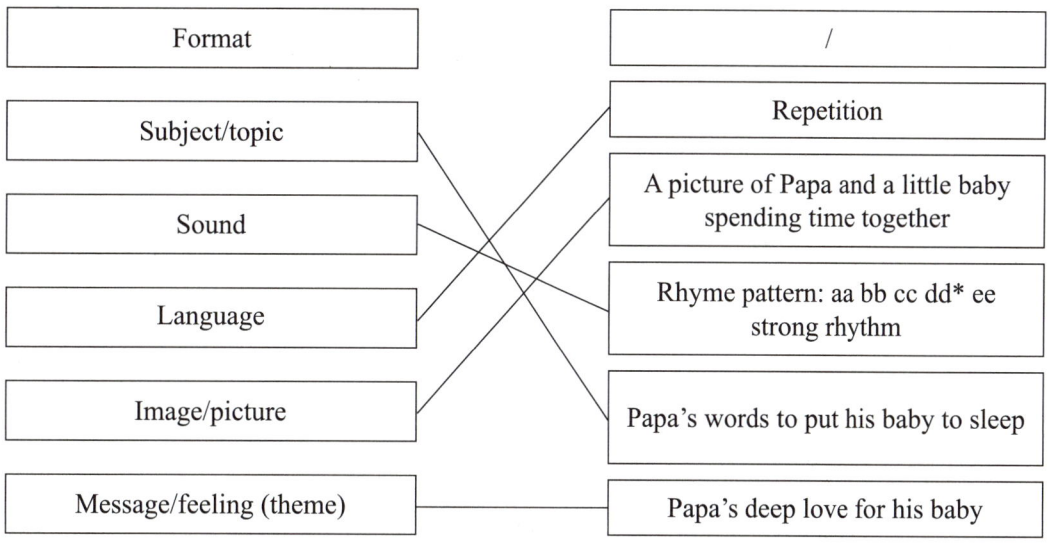

4. Read Paragraph 2, find the characteristics of nursery rhymes, and fill in the form.

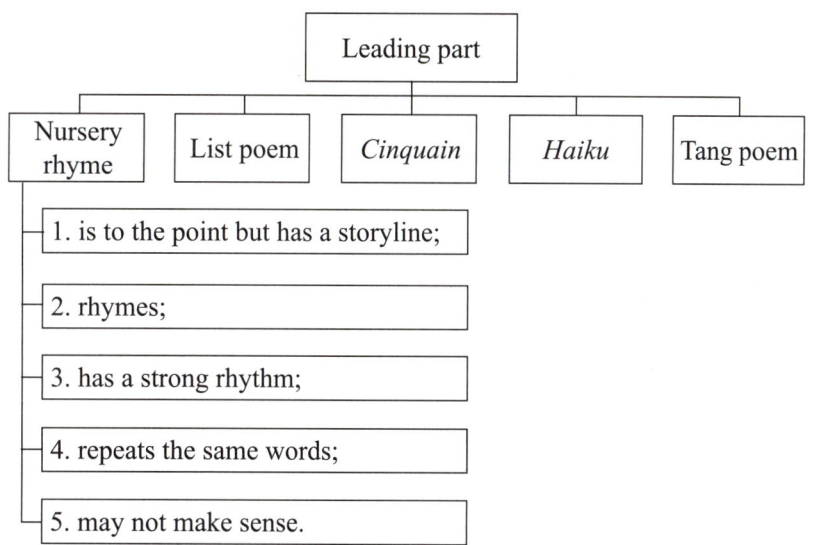

【设计意图】步骤1引导学生先不看说明性文字，直接读诗例A，感受童谣的特点。步骤2和步骤3让学生利用本课归纳出来的诗歌赏析维度对诗例A进行初步赏析。步骤4让学生回过头去看说明性文字，找出童谣类诗歌的特点，将自己的赏析和说明性文字进行比较，加深对童谣的理解。

【核心素养提升点】培养学生自主赏析诗歌的能力；提升学生查找重点信息的能力；提升学生的口头表达能力。

Activity 5: Learning about the list poem

本活动旨在落实课时目标4。

1. **Read Paragraph 3 and find the characteristics of the list poem.**

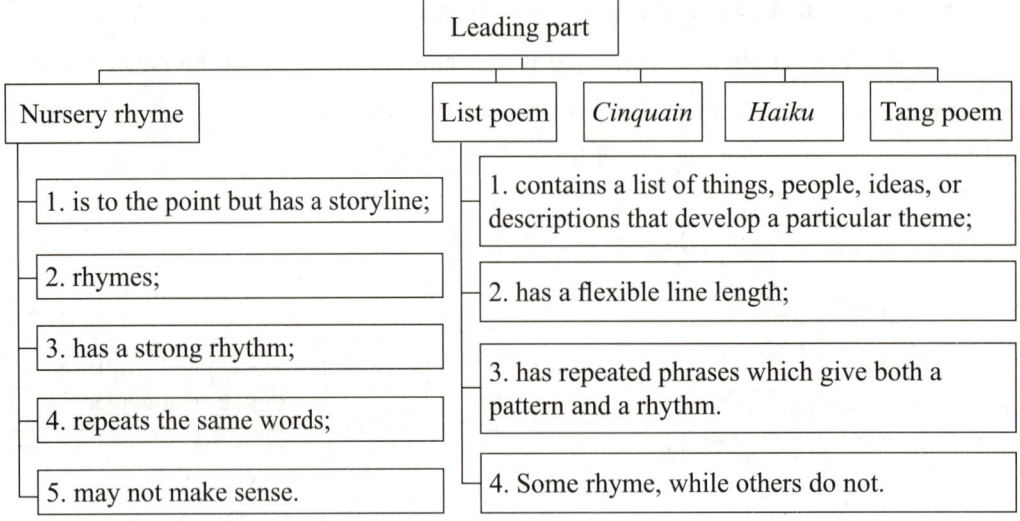

2. **Read Poem B and raise some questions about how to appreciate the poem.**

Q: If you were an English teacher, what questions would you ask your students to help them appreciate the poem?

(What feeling does the poem convey? / What literary devices are used in this poem? / What is the subject of the poem? / How does the poem sound? / What image does the poem create? ...)

3. **Discuss the questions with a partner and write down your answers in the table.**

Aspect	List poem	Poem B
Format	/	/
Subject/topic	/	Mother
Sound Language Image/picture	It contains a list of things, people, ideas, or descriptions; has a flexible line length and repeated phrases which give both a pattern and a rhythm to the poem. Some rhyme.	Rhyme (sky—by; together—weather; dawn—lawn; clover—over) Repetition, personification, contrast A list of beautiful and colourful images
Message/feeling (theme)	/	Love for one's mother

UNIT 5 POEMS

【设计意图】步骤1引导学生查找重点信息，整理相关语言表达，结合诗例准确理解生词。步骤2和步骤3引导学生利用这些信息和语言以及之前归纳的诗歌赏析维度，在教师的引领下自主探究诗例B，主动提问并尝试给出答案，然后进行几分钟的无干扰阅读和小组讨论，对诗例进行简单解读，巩固所学的赏析技能和词汇，加深对清单诗的理解。

【核心素养提升点】培养学生自主思考、主动提问的能力；提升学生的小组合作能力；提升学生的诗歌赏析能力。

Assignment

1. Read the rest of the text and finish the structure chart.
2. Read Poems A, B & C with emotion, and analyse Poem C, writing down key words in the table.

【设计意图】作业1让学生完成文本结构图，旨在训练其查找及提炼信息的能力。此外，填图的过程也是理解文本内容、梳理重要词汇的过程。作业2引导学生从朗读中体会诗歌的韵律及表达的情感，感受诗歌的美，明白朗读的重要性，培养课后朗读的习惯；让学生自行赏析诗例C（包括文本未收录的诗歌最后一节），旨在帮助学生巩固本节课所学的语言知识与赏析技能，培养学生自主赏析诗歌的能力。

【核心素养提升点】促进学生朗读习惯的养成；提升学生查找和提炼重要信息的能力；培养学生自主赏析诗歌的能力。

四、教学反思

本节课的目标主要是帮助学生初步了解诗人创作诗歌的原因及诗歌的类型和特点，并运用文本信息赏析相应诗例。导入部分激发了学生的兴趣，引出了与诗歌有关的词汇，帮助学生轻松且较好地实现课时目标1。在活动2中，教师带领学生解读文本首段，总结诗歌赏析维度，达成课时目标2的同时，为后续学习做好铺垫。在活动4中，教师让学生先不看说明性文字，尝试自主赏析诗例，这样可以确保真实的诗歌赏析体验。在活动5的自主提问环节，由于前面活动的铺垫，此处学生的提问较好地抓住了要点，并且学生能够自主回答这些问题。

从具体的教学环节看，本节课还存在一些需要改进的地方。第一，教师提问后多采用了学生集体回答的方式，虽然节省了时间，但没有照顾到部分想要回答问题的学生的需求。第二，在归纳诗歌赏析的六个维度时，教师说得偏多。为了培养学生的自主探究能力，教师可以尝试留下时间让学生自主归纳。第三，在学生分享自己对诗歌的理解后，教师立刻进行点评，虽然可以及时表扬或纠错，但也影响了学生表达的完整性。第四，诗例A并没有直接描绘父亲哄孩子睡觉的画面，这和后面几首诗例都不一样，教师最好能点出来。第五，在整个教学过程中，学生回答问题时组织语言的能力有些薄弱，需要教师进一步帮助和引导。第六，学生自主阅读和小组讨论的时间还不够充分。教师需要给予他们更多自主学习和合作学习的时间。

第二课时

一、课时目标

1. 分享对诗例C的赏析作业,复习诗歌赏析维度,通过总结五行诗、俳句和唐诗的特点,完善文本结构图。

2. 通过问题引领和小组讨论,抓住五行诗的特点,赏析诗例D;探究五行诗诗句的构成与功能,归纳创作规则,深化对五行诗的理解,同时复习定语从句的用法。

3. 在阅读中主动探究,抓住要点自主赏析俳句诗例,并用合适的语言进行书面表述。

4. 从打乱的诗句中整理出两首诗,从形式、内容两方面加深对五行诗和俳句的理解;通过对唐诗的赏析,巩固诗歌赏析维度,提升诗歌赏析能力和语言表达能力。

二、设计思路

本节课以帮助学生深入了解五行诗、俳句特征,赏析相应诗例的形式、内容和其传达的情感为重点展开。教师首先引导学生交流课后作业,分享自己对诗例C的赏析作业;接着引导学生补全五种诗歌形式的特点,完善文本结构图;之后引导学生针对诗例D,小组讨论并回答教师提出的几个问题,对诗例进行赏析,将答案整合成一段文字,并通过观察,归纳五行诗的创作规则,深化对五行诗的理解,同时复习定语从句;然后引导学生抓住俳句特点,自主赏析诗例E,补全赏析文字,操练相关语言;最后引导学生从打乱的诗句中整理出一首五行诗和一首俳句,并通过赏析了解这两首诗都以石妻为话题,自然过渡到唐诗赏析,并在课后完成赏析作业。学生在这一过程中进一步内化语言,提升诗歌赏析能力,培养逻辑思维能力和批判性思维能力。

三、教学过程

Activity 1: Reviewing the assignment

本活动旨在落实课时目标1。

1. Share and analyse your appreciation of Poem C.

Aspect	Poem C
Format	/
Subject/topic	*Life*
Sound Language Image/picture	*Rhyming words(bad—sad; thoughts—court)* *Repetition (Life can) and contrast (good & bad, cheerful & sad)*
Message/feeling (theme)	*Life is full of possibilities. It's up to you to make it better.*

2. List the characteristics of the *cinquain*, *haiku*, and Tang poem (the characteristics of Tang poem are not mentioned in the text).

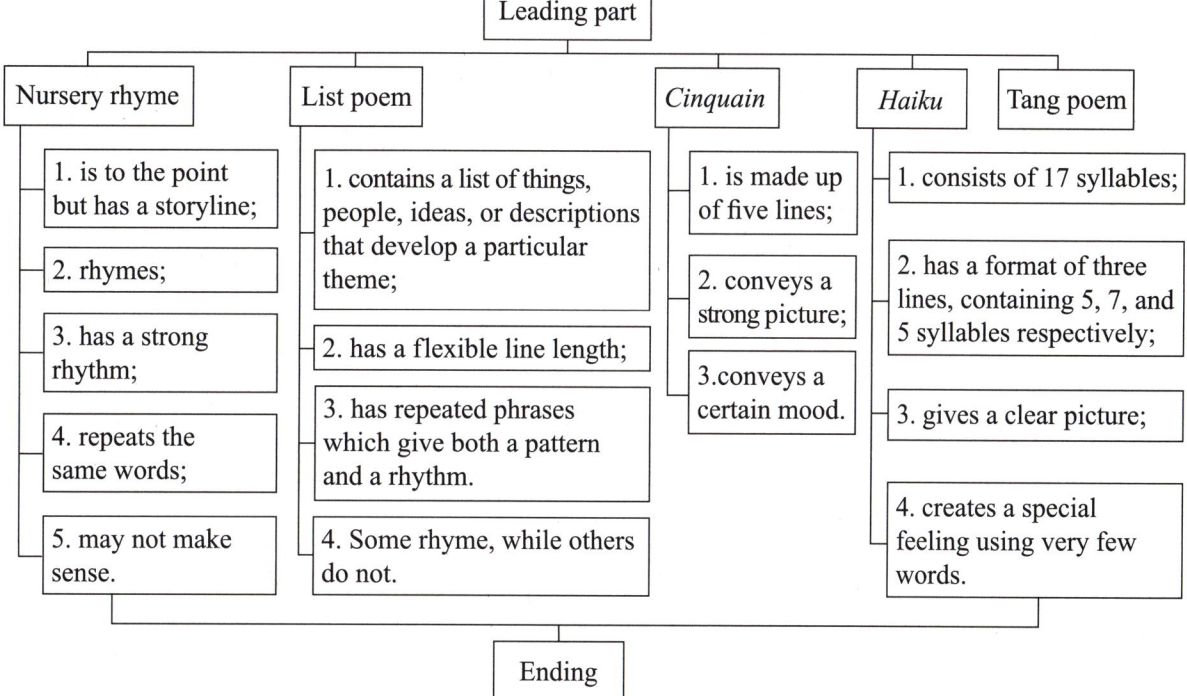

【设计意图】步骤1帮助学生回忆诗例C的内容，体会诗例传达的情感，并复习诗歌赏析维度。步骤2引导学生进一步完善第一课时整理出来的文本结构图，自然导入本节课要学习的诗歌形式。

【核心素养提升点】提升学生提取和组织信息的能力；培养学生的诗歌朗诵能力和赏析能力。

Activity 2: Appreciating Poem D

本活动旨在落实课时目标2。

1. Read Poem D and answer the following questions.

Q1: How many lines does the poem have?

Q2: What's the subject of this poem?

Q3: What picture does the poem convey?

Q4: What adjectives can be used to describe "brother"?

Q5: What mood does the poem convey?

2. Discuss the questions in pairs and finish the table.

Aspect	Cinquain	Poem D
Format	It is made up of five lines.	*Five lines*
Subject/topic	/	*My brother*

Aspect	Cinquain	Poem D
Sound **Language** **Image/picture**	It conveys a strong picture.	*Good-looking, naughty, noisy, energetic* *Playing crazily*
Message/feeling (theme)	It conveys a certain mood.	*Love, proud, angry, unhappy*

3. Fill in the blanks and turn the answers into a short paragraph.

(The poem has a format of <u>**five lines**</u>. The subject of this poem is <u>**brother**</u>. It conveys a strong picture of a <u>**good-looking, naughty, noisy, and energetic brother, playing crazily.**</u> It expresses a feeling that <u>the writer loves his/her brother and is proud of having such a brother, although sometimes he/she may be unhappy about his naughtiness.</u>)

4. Figure out the function of each line, and generalise it with attributive clauses.

The teacher explains the first line and the last line as examples.

Line 1 has one noun <u>that/which</u> is the subject of the poem (also the title of the poem).

Line 2 has two adjectives <u>that/which</u> describe the title.

Line 3 has three verbs ending in "-*ing*" <u>that/which</u> show the actions of the subject.

Line 4 has four words <u>that/which</u> show feelings about the subject.

Line 5 has one word <u>that/which</u> explains the subject.

【设计意图】步骤1和步骤2引导学生在和同伴讨论、回答问题的过程中，运用所学语言和诗歌赏析维度赏析诗例D，实践诗歌赏析的方法。步骤3引导学生将问题的答案整合成一小段文字，进一步巩固和内化相关语言。步骤4让学生观察五行诗，模仿教师给出的例子，探究和理解五行诗每一行诗句的功能，并且运用定语从句进行归纳，旨在锻炼学生的观察能力、归纳能力和表达能力，同时帮助学生复习定语从句的用法。

【核心素养提升点】培养学生自主思考、主动提问的能力；培养学生的小组合作能力；提升学生的观察和归纳能力；提升学生的语言表达能力。

Activity 3: Appreciating Poem E

本活动旨在落实课时目标3。

1. Read Poem E together, count the syllables, and enjoy a painting about the poem.

2. Appreciate Poem E and fill in the blanks. Discuss with a partner, if necessary.

- The poem has a format of ____ lines, containing _____ syllables respectively.
- The subject of this poem is _____.
- It creates a vivid picture in my mind that _____.
- I can sense a strong feeling from the poem that _____.

(The poem has a format of **3** lines, containing **5, 7, and 5** syllables respectively. The subject of this poem is **a butterfly**. It creates a vivid picture in my mind that **a flower-like butterfly flies freely through blossoms and rests on a branch**. I can sense a strong feeling from the poem that **the writer appreciates the beauty of nature. He/she feels amazed at the sight.**)

【设计意图】步骤1引导学生朗读诗例E，欣赏相关图片，直观感受诗例所传递的画面，深刻理解诗中的意象。步骤2引导学生利用诗歌赏析维度自主赏析诗例E，抓住俳句特点，用自己的语言描述诗例传递的画面，挖掘诗例蕴含的情感内涵。

【核心素养提升点】提升学生理解诗歌蕴含的情感内涵的能力；提升学生的语言表达能力；培养学生的小组合作能力。

Activity 4: Reviewing the text and sorting out the poems

本活动旨在落实课时目标4。

1. Put the lines of a *cinquain* and a *haiku* in the correct order.

T: I once heard a story that happened in ancient times. A woman's husband joined the army and never came back. The woman stood on the riverside waiting for him day after day, until she eventually turned to stone. I composed two poems on this topic, a *cinquain* and a *haiku*, but I put the lines in an incorrect order. Put the lines of each poem into the correct order.

Wife Hopeful, faithful Waiting, staring, expecting Love is solid like Stone	Who's waiting for love? Rain or shine, windy or fine. There stands a stone wife!

2. Read Poem F and answer some questions about it.

T: Just like Poem D and Poem E, Poem F also conveys a strong picture and a special feeling.

Q1: What is the subject of this poem?

Q2: What picture does this poem convey?

Q3: What feelings (the stone wife's feelings and the poet's feelings) does this poem convey?

Aspect	Poem F
Format	/
Subject/topic	*A stone wife*
Sound Language Image/picture	*It conveys a picture of a stone wife standing on top of a mountain, staring at a river and waiting for her husband to come back.*
Message/feeling(theme)	*The poem expresses the wife's strong love and longing for her husband. It also expresses the poet's great sympathy and admiration for the faithful stone wife.*

【设计意图】步骤1引导学生从杂乱的句子中找出分别属于两首诗的诗句，并按照已掌握的五行诗和俳句的诗歌形式、韵律等知识，将这些诗句进行排序，把它们重新组成完整的五行诗和俳句，旨在帮助学生巩固五行诗和俳句的特点，加深对这两类诗歌的理解。步骤2引导学生利用所学，自主赏析唐诗诗例，巩固诗歌赏析维度。

【核心素养提升点】培养学生整合诗句的能力；加深学生对英语诗歌文化的理解；提升学生的诗歌赏析能力。

Assignment

Write a short passage to appreciate Poem F. You may use some of the following sentence structures.

- The subject/topic of this poem is _____.
- The poem has _____ lines.
- When I read the poem aloud, I can hear that the words _____ rhyme, which makes the poem pleasing to read.
- It conveys a strong picture of _____.
- Line ___ uses a literary device—_____.
- The words _____ are impressive because _____.
- It expresses/conveys a feeling of _____.
- I think the poem sends us a message: _____.

【设计意图】引导学生将课堂上口头赏析的内容落实到书面，以文本输出的方式综合运用话题语言和诗歌赏析维度，有效巩固两节课所学。考虑到学生的英语水平，教师应提供相关句式，适当搭建语言支架，帮助学生在实践中内化相关语言。

【核心素养提升点】提升学生自主赏析诗歌的能力；提升学生的书面表达能力；培养学生的批判性思维能力。

The teacher's version:

The subject of this poem is a stone wife. Containing eight lines, the poem conveys a strong picture of a stone wife standing on top of a mountain, staring at a river and waiting for her husband to come back. The literary device personification is used and the phrases "on and on" and "day by day" are impressive because these words indicate a long distance and long time. The poem conveys the poet's strong sympathy and admiration for those women whose husbands were far away in the army, and he sang high praise for their unfailing love.

四、教学反思

本节课整体上较好地实现了教学目标。课堂活动从教师问题引领到学生自主赏析，层层深入，过程较为顺畅，目标达成情况较好。首先，教师通过分享一位学生对诗例C的赏析，带领全班一起回顾了诗歌赏析维度。然后教师引导学生通过图表总结五种诗歌形式的特点，有效整合了关键信息。接下来，教师引导学生通过小组讨论、自主观察、主动探究等方式，赏析不同的诗例，感受这几类诗歌的魅力，同时复习了定语从句。在活动3中，教师利用多媒体技术呈现了蝴蝶在花丛中飞舞的画面，既激发了学生的兴趣，也让学生在赏析诗歌时更有代入感。活动4的设计巧妙，帮助学生既巩固了前面所学又自然过渡到唐诗赏析。课后作业提供了语言支架，促进学生巩固和内化所学语言和诗歌知识。

　　本节课存在几点不足之处。第一，活动2中关于诗例D的问题是由教师提出的。如果时间允许，教师可以让学生通过讨论，自主提出关于诗歌赏析的问题。第二，因为课时所限，学生对唐诗的赏析不够充分，只能在课后作业中进行弥补。第三，整节课在语言方面的铺垫还有不足，导致学生回答问题时有不少地方需要教师引导，缺少整段的输出。第四，如果时间允许，教师在活动3呈现学生的作品后，最好先让其他学生进行点评和补充。

第三节 提高版教学案例

教学内容安排：第一课时引导学生理解全文，重点研读文本第一至第三段，赏析两首诗例；第二课时引导学生研读文本第四至第七段，再品读三首诗例，并根据诗歌特点进行诗歌创作和赏析。

第一课时

一、课时目标

1. 解读文本第一段，提炼诗歌的基本要素及诗歌赏析维度。
2. 通过略读、扫读和自主提问，梳理文本结构，获取文本基本信息和文体特征，了解举例子的说明方法。
3. 通过阅读定位重要信息，把握童谣特点，深入赏析童谣诗例。
4. 通过小组合作阅读，对清单诗诗例进行赏析和讨论，内化相关语言，培养自主学习能力。

二、设计思路

教师首先用自己所作的诗歌导入话题，引出并解释一些与诗歌音韵和话题相关的词汇，如 rhyme、syllable、rhythm、subject 等，为课堂词汇运用和诗例赏析做好铺垫；其次让学生阅读文本第一段，找出该段的两个关键词 reasons 和 characteristics，并提取相关信息，从形式、内容和意义三个方面归纳诗歌赏析的六个维度；接着引导学生进行读中预测活动，根据标题和第一段最后一句话判断下文走向；随后引导学生自主探究，从内容到行文方式提出自己认为重要的问题并尝试给出答案，再进行无干扰阅读，梳理文本结构并画出文本结构图；然后引导学生细读第二段，查找童谣的基本特征，并在问题引领下赏析诗例；最后让学生细读第三段，找出清单诗的主要特征，小组合作自主赏析其中一首诗例，思考诗例传达的思想感情。课后作业是让学生针对两首清单诗写下100词左右的诗歌赏析文段，旨在帮助学生内化所学语言，培养思维能力。

三、教学过程

Activity 1: Activating background knowledge related to poems

本活动为实现课时目标1做铺垫。

Read *My Cat* and clap the rhythm.

T: I am an English poetry amateur. An amateur is someone who does something as a hobby and not as a job. I'm very glad and honoured to introduce to you my masterpiece. The subject or topic of this poem is "cat". Let's read it and clap the rhythm.

My cat
I once had a cat
Never catching a rat
Always lying on a mat
No wonder he was fat

Q1: What makes the poem sound good?

Q2: What are "rhythm" and "rhyme"?

(<u>Rhythm</u> is a regular pattern of sounds, containing strong and weak syllables. A <u>syllable</u> is a unit of pronunciation which has one vowel sound. In poems, the words at the ends of the lines often sound very similar; these words are called <u>rhyming words</u>. Rhyme, syllable, and rhythm form the sound of a poem.)

> 【设计意图】引导学生通过朗诵教师创作的《我的猫》这首诗，感知文本话题，激发学习兴趣，同时了解英语诗歌的部分基本要素和赏析维度——subject/topic 和 sound（rhyme、syllable、rhythm）；引导学生重点学习部分新词汇，如 amateur、rhyme、syllable、rhythm 等，为后文阅读做好准备。
>
> 【核心素养提升点】提升学生对英语诗歌韵律和节奏的理解。

Activity 2: Identifying the text type and noting the aspects of poem appreciation

本活动旨在落实课时目标1。

1. Identify the text type.

(Exposition.)

2. Locate the two key words in the first paragraph.

(Reasons and characteristics.)

3. Find the reasons why people compose poetry.

(Some poems tell a story or describe a certain image in the reader's mind. Others try to convey certain feelings such as joy and sorrow.)

T: Basically, poets write poems to "express themselves", which means to convey a message or a certain feeling. Messages and feelings form the theme of the poem.

4. Find the characteristics of English poetry.

(The distinctive characteristics of English poetry often include economical use of words, descriptive and vivid language, integrated imagery, literary devices such as similes and metaphors, and arrangement of words, lines, rhymes, and rhythm.)

5. Note the aspects of poem appreciation.

Form	Format	arrangement of words, lines, rhymes, and rhythm
Content	Subject/topic	/
	Sound	rhyme, syllable, rhythm
	Language	economical use of words, descriptive and vivid language, literary devices
	Image/picture	integrated imagery
Meaning	Message/feeling (theme)	Poets use many different forms of poetry to express themselves.

【设计意图】步骤1让学生判断文本类型，旨在培养学生的文体意识，同时为后面引导学生关注文本说明方法做铺垫。步骤2至步骤4带领学生阅读首段，找出关键信息，即作诗原因和诗歌特点；引导学生理解生词含义，挖掘词汇内涵，并在此基础上归纳诗歌赏析的四大维度。步骤5引导学生结合读前活动中所引入的两个维度，总结完整的诗歌赏析六维度，为解读后文的诗例做准备。

【核心素养提升点】培养学生主动思考的能力；提升学生查找、提取、整合关键信息的能力。

Activity 3: Predicting the text content and drawing the structure of the text

本活动旨在落实课时目标2。

1. Put forward some questions about the rest of the text that you consider important.

Q1: According to the title and the last sentence of the first paragraph, what will be talked about in the rest of the text?

(Some forms of English poetry.)

Q2: If you were the writer, what writing technique or method would you use to introduce the forms?

(Giving examples.)

T: Before reading the rest of the text, based on your prediction, put forward some questions about the rest of the text that you consider important. For example, how many forms are introduced?

Question you would like to ask	Your answer
1. How many forms are introduced?	
2. What forms are introduced?	

续表

Question you would like to ask	Your answer
3. How many example poems are given?	
4. Which poems are used to explain each form?	
5. What are the characteristics of each form?	
6. How do we appreciate these poems?	

2. Read the text to see if you can find the answers, and then share some of the answers.
3. Draw the structure of the text.

【设计意图】让学生根据标题和首段过渡句预测后文内容，在初步预测的基础上以提问的形式思考后文会涉及的主要方面，在寻找答案的过程中搜索关键词句，厘清文本脉络，画出文本结构图。

【核心素养提升点】培养学生合理预测、主动提问的能力；培养学生梳理文本结构的能力；提升学生的逻辑思维能力。

Activity 4: Identifying the detailed information

本活动旨在落实课时目标3。

1. Read Paragraph 2 and find the characteristics of the nursery rhyme.

Aspect	Nursery rhyme	Poem A
Format	/	/
Subject/topic	/	
Sound Language Image/picture	*The language of it is to the point but has a storyline. It rhymes; has a strong rhythm; repeats the same words; may not make sense.*	
Message/feeling (theme)	/	

2. Read Poem A and clap the rhythm. Answer the following questions with your partner.

Q1: What is the father doing?

Q2: What are the rhyming words?

Q3: What literary device is used?

Q4: Does the storyline make sense? Why?

Q5: What feeling does the poem convey?

Aspect	Nursery rhyme	Poem A
Format	/	/
Subject/topic	/	Papa's words to put his baby to sleep
Sound Language Image/picture	The language of it is to the point but has a storyline. It rhymes; has a strong rhythm; repeats the same words; may not make sense.	Rhyme (word—bird; sing—ring; brass—glass; broke—goat; pull—bull) Strong rhythm Repetition to the point; storyline (does not make sense)
Message/feeling (theme)	/	Papa's deep love for his baby

3. Fill in the blanks to consolidate.

The topic of the nursery rhyme is a father's words to put his baby to sleep. The _____ words include word—bird, sing—ring, brass—glass, broke—goat, pull—bull. In other words, every two lines _____. The poem has a strong _____. The language is concrete and _____. _____ is the main literary device in this poem. Besides this, there is a storyline, but it does not _____ since it is unlikely that a father would buy all those gifts for his baby. This poem conveys the feeling that _____.

【设计意图】步骤1引导学生总结童谣的特点，学习与童谣有关的语言表达。步骤2引导学生利用这些信息和语言以及六大诗歌赏析维度，在问题的引领下对诗例A进行赏析。步骤3引导学生补全针对诗例A的赏析小文段，巩固所学的赏析技能和词汇，加深对童谣的理解。

【核心素养提升点】培养学生查找重点信息的能力；提升学生的诗歌赏析能力。

Activity 5: Practising the techniques to appreciate the list poem

本活动旨在落实课时目标4。

1. Read Paragraph 3 and find the characteristics of the list poem.

Aspect	List poem	Poem C
Format	/	/
Subject/topic	/	
Sound **Language** **Image/picture**	*It contains a list of things, people, ideas, or descriptions that develop a particular theme. It has a flexible line length and repeated phrases which give both a pattern and a rhythm to the poem. Some rhyme.*	
Message/feeling (theme)	/	

2. **Read Poem C and discuss in groups of four how to appreciate this poem. Write down some key words.**

Aspect	List poem	Poem C
Format	/	/
Subject/topic	/	*Life*
Sound **Language** **Image/picture**	It contains a list of things, people, ideas, or descriptions that develop a particular theme. It has a flexible line length and repeated phrases which give both a pattern and a rhythm to the poem. Some rhyme.	*Rhyme (bad—sad; thoughts—court);* *Repetition is used to give the poem a pattern.* *A list of adjectives and important things in life are used to make a contrast.*
Message/feeling (theme)	/	*Life is full of possibilities and it's up to you to decide what your life will be like. Try to make it better.*

【设计意图】引导学生查找重点信息，整理相关语言表达，并利用这些信息和语言以及六大诗歌赏析维度，通过小组合作对诗例C进行赏析，尤其要感悟诗歌所传达的主题思想——人生充满不确定性，每个人要积极面对自己的人生，努力活出价值、活出品质，从而获得积极的人生体验。

> 【核心素养提升点】培养学生自主思考的能力；提升学生小组合作学习的能力；提升学生的口头表达能力。

Assignment

Write an appreciation of Poem B or Poem C in around 100 words.

> 【设计意图】让学生针对诗例B或诗例C写下100词左右的赏析文段，将课堂上口头赏析的内容落实到书面，及时巩固课堂所学的词汇和相关语言结构，提升诗歌赏析水平和书面表达能力。
>
> 【核心素养提升点】培养学生的诗歌赏析能力；提升学生的词汇运用和写作能力。

The teacher's version:

Version 1:

The subject of this list poem is mother. The rhyming words are sky—by, together—weather, dawn—lawn, and clover—over. The literary devices used in this poem include repetition (hundreds of), contrast (hundreds of—only one), and personification (dewdrops to greet the dawn). The poem contains a list of beautiful and colourful natural sights, but all these sights fade in comparison to a mother. It conveys a strong feeling of love for one's mother.

Version 2:

The topic of Poem C is life. The second line and fourth line rhyme (bad—sad), and so do the sixth line and eighth line (thoughts—court). The poem contains a list of adjectives about life (good—bad, cheerful—sad) and things in life (dreams, great thoughts—sitting in court), which form a contrast. Repetition is another literary device used in the poem (Life can ...). Through this poem, the poet conveys the message that life is full of possibilities and it's up to everyone to decide what his or her life will be like.

四、教学反思

本节课将学生自主阅读、探究学习与教师引领相结合，较好地实现了教学目标。学生通过本节课的学习，能够了解诗人创作诗歌的原因及五种诗歌形式的特点，并利用文本信息，总结诗歌赏析维度，运用所学赏析诗例。整节课教学目标明确，主线清晰，层次分明，从学习理解、整理归纳到应用实践、内化运用，每一步都在为后面的步骤做铺垫。导入环节简单高效，激活学生已知的同时处理了几个关键生词。活动2中学生对第一段的解读比较到位，教师在此基础上引导学生整合信息，带领学生归纳了诗歌赏析的六大维度，并在此过程中解释了一些与诗歌有关的词汇，学生理解得也比较好。学生自主阅读和提问环节难度较高，但还是有学生可以抓住要点进行提问。在提出问题和解决问题的过程中，教师适时地针对部分学生的回答进行纠正和引导，有效地帮助学生加深对诗歌的理解。在最后一个环节，学生能较好地利用诗歌赏析维度进行诗歌赏析。该诗歌赏析在课后作业中落实到了书面，进一步锻炼了学生的书面表达能力。

本节课在具体的教学环节方面还存在一些需要改进的地方。第一，在归纳诗歌赏析的六大维度时，教师说得偏多。教师可以尝试留下时间让学生自主归纳。第二，在自主提问环节，教师引导得还不够，导致学生思维比较局限，提出的一些问题比较杂乱或者重复，问不到重点。有些比较好的问题，如"Who wrote these poems?""How do we write a poem of a certain form?"都没有被提及。第三，整节课教师对课堂的掌控偏多，学生自主交流与讨论的时间偏少。建议在自主提问和最后的诗例 C 赏析环节，教师给予学生更多思考和讨论的时间。第四，教师对于赏析诗歌时所用语言的整理还不够，导致部分学生写赏析文段时语言比较贫乏。教师应引导学生进一步整理和归纳话题语言，帮助学生丰富相关的语言表达。

第二课时

一、课时目标

1. 分享诗歌赏析作业，复习诗歌赏析维度，巩固内化语言。

2. 通过自主阅读，用自己的语言描述三首诗所传递的画面并阐述作者所要传达的情感，培养自主学习能力和语言表达能力。

3. 观察五行诗行文特点，归纳五行诗创作规则，提升观察能力和归纳能力；通过逐句朗读划分音节，理解俳句的音节分布模式，提升对诗歌音韵的理解。

4. 整理创作步骤，通过创作诗歌，体验创作过程，深化对诗歌诸要素的理解，提升创造性思维能力和语言表达能力。

二、设计思路

本节课教师首先讲评上节课布置的作业，通过分享学生及教师自己对诗例B和诗例C的赏析，帮助学生回顾诗歌赏析的六大维度，巩固相关语言，为接下来的赏析做好铺垫；其次让学生不看说明性文字直接快速阅读五行诗、俳句和唐诗的三个诗例，寻找这三首诗的共性；接着引导学生通过自主探究的方式进行无干扰阅读，仔细品读这三个诗例，用自己的语言概括每首诗传递了什么画面，抒发了作者怎样的情感；随后引导学生着重分析五行诗的格式特征，找寻五行诗创作规则；然后让学生通过逐句分析俳句的格式尤其是音节分布模式，适当了解俳句的背景信息，拓展知识面；最后带领学生总结诗歌的创作流程，引导学生根据一幅图画，创作一首五行诗或俳句，体验诗歌的创作过程，深入感受诗歌各要素在诗歌创作中的有机结合。学生完成创作后，教师可选择若干作品让学生赏析，帮助学生内化所学语言和诗歌知识。课后作业让学生选择感兴趣的人或物，用本单元所学的任意一种诗歌形式写一首诗并进行自我赏析。这个作业给予学生充分的创作自由，不仅可以提升学生的创造性思维能力和语言表达能力，也能进一步提升他们的诗歌赏析能力。

三、教学过程

Activity 1: Reviewing what has been learnt

本活动旨在落实课时目标1。

1. Share some appreciations of Poem B and Poem C with the whole class.
2. Read the teacher's appreciations of the two poems.

【设计意图】引导学生通过分享赏析作业，回顾诗歌赏析的六大维度，巩固和内化语言，为接下来的赏析做好准备。

【核心素养提升点】提升学生的语言表达能力；培养学生的诗歌赏析能力。

Activity 2: Appreciating Poem D, Poem E, and Poem F

本活动旨在落实课时目标2。

Read poems D, E, and F with emotion, and appreciate the three poems.

Q1: What are the subjects of the three poems?

Q2: Among the six appreciation aspects, which two aspects of these three poems impress you most?

T: All these three poems convey/give a strong/clear picture and convey/create a certain mood / special feeling. What image and feeling does each of the poems convey? Please describe each image in one sentence in your own words, and write down the feeling it conveys.

Aspect	Poem D	Poem E	Poem F
Subject/topic	Brother	A butterfly	A stone wife
Image/picture	The poem gives a strong picture of a good-looking, naughty, noisy, and energetic brother, playing crazily.	The poem conveys a picture that a butterfly, which looks like a blossom, flies up and rests on a branch.	It conveys a picture of a stone woman standing on top of a mountain, staring at a river and waiting for her husband to come back.
Message/feeling	It expresses a feeling that the writer loves his/her brother and is proud of having such a brother, although sometimes he/she may be unhappy about his naughtiness.	It shows the writer's amazement and admiration for the beautiful sight in nature.	The poem expresses the wife's strong love and longing for her husband. It also expresses the poet's great sympathy and admiration for the faithful stone wife.

【设计意图】引导学生不看说明性文字，直接快速阅读五行诗、俳句和唐诗的三个诗例，寻找这三首诗的共性，即三首诗都传递了一个清晰的画面，表达了作者强烈的情感；引导学生通过自主探究的方式进行无干扰阅读，仔细品读这三个诗例，用自己的语言概括每首诗传递了什么画面，抒发了怎样的情感。这个过程既锻炼了学生的诗歌赏析能力，也培养了他们的书面表达能力。

【核心素养提升点】提升学生的书面表达能力；培养学生主动思考的能力；培养学生的批判性思维能力。

Activity 3: Learning about the format of the *cinquain* and the *haiku*

本活动旨在落实课时目标3。

1. Read Paragraph 4 with Poem D and answer the following questions.

Q1: What are the characteristics of the *cinquain*?

(The *cinquain* is made up of five lines. It conveys a strong picture or a certain mood in just a few words.)

Q2: How many lines does a *cinquain* contain?

(A *cinquain* contains five lines.)

Q3: How is each line formed? What is the function of each line?

T: For example, the first line is a noun, which is the subject of the poem. The fifth line is one specific word that explains the subject. Please read these two examples and figure out the functions of the other three lines.

(The second line contains two adjectives that describe the subject. The third line has three verbs ending in "*-ing*" that describe actions relating to the subject. The fourth line is a four-word phrase that describes a feeling relating to the subject.)

2. Read Paragraph 5 and pay attention to the expository technique—giving definitions. Read Poem E and learn the syllable structure of a *haiku*.

T: The first sentence of Paragraph 5 has a typical definition structure with the sentence pattern "... is / refers to ... poem/poetry that ...".

Let's read the poem together and find out how many syllables each line contains.

A fall-en blos-som
Is com-ing back to the branch.
Look, a but-ter-fly!

3. Supply some extra information about *haiku* poems.

T: A *haiku* contains concrete images and descriptions. It is written in the present tense, and a good *haiku* usually ends with a surprising last line.

【设计意图】步骤1引导学生阅读第四段说明性文字及诗例D，着重分析五行诗的格式特征，观察诗歌行文特点，找寻五行诗的创作规则，锻炼观察能力和归纳能力，为之后的诗歌创作做好准备。步骤2和步骤3引导学生阅读第五段说明性文字和诗例E，掌握下定义的说明方法，再逐句分析俳句的音节分布模式，适当了解俳句的背景信息，增加相关知识储备，为之后的诗歌创作打下基础。

【核心素养提升点】提升学生查找重点信息的能力；提升学生主动思考的能力；培养学生的归纳概括能力。

Activity 4: Practising poem writing and appreciating

本活动旨在落实课时目标4。

1. List the steps of writing a poem.

(1) Decide on a subject/topic and make sure what message or feeling you want to convey.

(2) Choose a form and think of the format.

(3) Think about the words, phrases, and literary devices you would like to use. Make your poem rhyme and give it a rhythm if you want.

(4) Check how well the details paint a picture in your head, and write it down.

(5) Read it aloud to yourself or your friends and make some improvements.

2. Write a *cinquain* or a *haiku* based on a picture.

3. Share and appreciate some poems.

> **A student's poem:**
> Mother
> Beautiful, gentle
> Smiling, hugging, protecting
> Best shelter for me
> Mine
>
> **The teacher's poems:**
> Daughter
> Cute, innocent
> Smiling, kissing, snuggling
> Just like an angel
> Mine
>
> The child's smiling face,
> Reminds me the warmest place
> Is Mother's embrace.

【设计意图】步骤1引导学生通过总结诗歌的创作流程，厘清诗歌创作思路，提高诗歌创作能力，为下一步完整创作诗歌搭建支架。步骤2引导学生实践上一步总结的诗歌创作流程，自主明确主题、建构意象、遣词造句、抒发情感，从赏析诗歌上升到创作诗歌，深化对诗歌诸要素的理解，将所学的相关知识应用于实践，体验诗歌的创作过程。步骤3引导学生赏析同伴作品，巩固诗歌赏析的方法。

【核心素养提升点】帮助学生加深对诗歌文化的理解；培养学生的创造性思维能力；提升学生的语言表达能力；提升学生的诗歌赏析能力。

Assignment

Choose a form of poem from this unit, write a poem about any subject you like, and analyse your poem using the following table.

Aspect		Poem appreciation & analysis
Form	Format	
Content	Subject/topic	
	Sound Language Image/picture	
Meaning	Message/feeling (theme)	

【设计意图】引导学生独立完整地创作诗歌，将诗歌文化知识与语言知识、书面写作技能相结合，锻炼构思、组织和表达等能力；引导学生分析自己创作的诗歌，回顾诗歌赏析的六大维度，进一步提升诗歌赏析能力。

【核心素养提升点】培养学生的诗歌创作能力；培养学生的创造性思维能力；提升学生的诗歌赏析能力。

The teacher's version:

    My cat
  I once had a cat
  Never catching a rat
  Always lying on a mat
  No wonder he was fat

The topic of this poem is a cat the poet had in the past. It contains four lines and all the lines rhyme. In each line, a strong syllable is followed by a weak syllable, which gives the poem a strong rhythm and makes it pleasing to read. The poem conveys a picture of a fat, lazy cat lying on a mat, but it also creates a feeling that the poet loves and misses the cat.

四、教学反思

本节课围绕培养学生诗歌赏析能力这一核心目标展开，从赏析到创作再到赏析，层次分明，重点突出。在活动2中，教师让学生先读诗歌再看说明性文字，使学生避免了被说明性文字限制住思维，帮助他们更真实地感受诗歌。同时，教师抓住三类诗歌的共同点将三个诗例打通教学。这种方式既突出了诗歌的特点又提高了课堂效率。在活动3中，教师引导学生通过自主探究的方式，感受五行诗的格式特征以及俳句的音节分布特点。在活动4中，教师给学生提供了创作支架，照顾了基础较弱的学生，也使基础好的学生能够创作出质量较高的诗歌。同时，大部分学生能抓住诗歌的主要特点以及诗歌赏析维度进行诗歌赏析。

本节课还存在一些需要改进的地方。第一，由于时间关系，对诗例B的解读只是在点评作业环节一带而过，显得有些仓促。第二，留给学生创作诗歌的时间还不够，课堂上也没有时间让学生进行交流和讨论。学生只能在课后去做这些活动。虽有部分学生创作的诗歌质量较高，但还是有不少学生组织语言的能力有些薄弱，需要教师进一步帮助和引导。第三，活动4中教师直接呈现了创作诗歌的几个步骤。建议教师引导学生自主讨论和总结诗歌创作流程，提高他们的自主学习和合作学习能力。第四，学生进行诗歌赏析时，教师的点评虽然有助于及时纠正问题，但也打断了学生发言的连续性。在时间允许的情况下，教师可以尝试先让学生完整地表述，然后请其他学生进行点评，最后再由教师进行点评。